CW01270740

Archangel Uriel

Connecting with the Angel of Wisdom

© Copyright 2024 - All rights reserved.

The content contained within this book may not be reproduced, duplicated, or transmitted without direct written permission from the author or the publisher.

Under no circumstances will any blame or legal responsibility be held against the publisher, or author, for any damages, reparation, or monetary loss due to the information contained within this book, either directly or indirectly.

Legal Notice:

This book is copyright protected. It is only for personal use. You cannot amend, distribute, sell, use, quote, or paraphrase any part of the content within this book without the consent of the author or publisher.

Disclaimer Notice:

Please note the information contained within this document is for educational and entertainment purposes only. All effort has been executed to present accurate, up-to-date, reliable, and complete information. No warranties of any kind are declared or implied. Readers acknowledge that the author is not engaging in the rendering of legal, financial, medical, or professional advice. The content within this book has been derived from various sources. Please consult a licensed professional before attempting any techniques outlined in this book.

By reading this document, the reader agrees that under no circumstances is the author responsible for any losses, direct or indirect, that are incurred as a result of the use of the information contained within this document, including, but not limited to, errors, omissions, or inaccuracies.

Your Free Gift
(only available for a limited time)

Thanks for getting this book! If you want to learn more about various spirituality topics, then join Mari Silva's community and get a free guided meditation MP3 for awakening your third eye. This guided meditation mp3 is designed to open and strengthen ones third eye so you can experience a higher state of consciousness. Simply visit the link below the image to get started.

https://spiritualityspot.com/meditation

Table of Contents

INTRODUCTION 1
CHAPTER 1: WHO IS ARCHANGEL URIEL? 3
CHAPTER 2: INVOKING ARCHANGEL URIEL............................... 13
CHAPTER 3: SIGNS OF URIEL'S PRESENCE.................................. 23
CHAPTER 4: CREATING ANGELIC SACRED SPACE 34
CHAPTER 5: SOLAR CHAKRA MEDITATION 44
CHAPTER 6: FIRE-IN-PALM MEDITATION 54
CHAPTER 7: DREAMWORK 64
CHAPTER 8: CRYSTALS AND CANDLES... 75
CHAPTER 9: DAILY RITUALS AND EXERCISES 87
BONUS: CORRESPONDENCES SHEET 95
CONCLUSION 97
HERE'S ANOTHER BOOK BY MARI SILVA THAT YOU MIGHT LIKE.... 99
YOUR FREE GIFT (ONLY AVAILABLE FOR A LIMITED TIME).............. 100
REFERENCES 101

Introduction

Have you ever been curious about Archangel Uriel and his powerful gifts? Do you want to become close with one of God's most influential Archangels? If so, this book is for you.

Archangel Uriel is an uplifting figure that fills people with joy and hope. His bright, shining light inspires his followers to see the world positively, even amid challenging times. As one of the four archangels, Uriel is known for his wisdom, creativity, and enlightenment. He is also associated with the element of fire, which represents transformation and passion. Whether you pray to him for guidance or simply feel his presence around you, Archangel Uriel is a powerful force for good in the world.

Worshiped and invoked by many in the Christian faith, Uriel can be called upon to help you in your spiritual journey. He can answer questions that bother you, inspire and help you develop your creative talents, or guide you toward manifesting success in your life. Invoking his presence can bring a sense of peace and balance, allowing you to feel more grounded and connected to the higher realms. Drawing energy from the sun, Uriel is a powerful light and healing source, reminding us of a benevolent divine power. For those looking to deepen their relationship with Archangel Uriel, this book will explain the spiritual and practical tools necessary for invocation.

There are ways to invoke Archangel Uriel and connect with him on a deeper level. But before you do, learn more about him, his energy, and how to create a sacred space for your connection. That's why this book is broken down into nine chapters. This descriptive guide will explore who Archangel Uriel is and examine his characteristics. This book will discuss how to invoke Uriel and recognize signs of his presence. It will also provide step-by-step instructions for creating an angelic sacred space and teach you various meditations, dreamwork techniques, and rituals to connect with Uriel.

This guide includes a bonus correspondence sheet that helps you better understand Uriel's traits and the energies he works with. Through this book, you'll understand what an archangel is, better understand Archangel Uriel, and learn how to create a strong connection with him. The guidance and wisdom he has to offer are sure to make your spiritual journey more rewarding. By reading this book and following the steps, you'll have all the information you need to work with Archangel Uriel. From here, you'll feel His presence in your life and benefit from the power of His light. So, let's get started and learn more about this magnificent archangel!

Chapter 1: Who Is Archangel Uriel?

Out of all the angels in the celestial realms, Archangel Uriel stands out as one of the most powerful and influential figures. He is renowned for his wisdom, justice, and strength across the angelic kingdom. Archangel Uriel plays an important role in communicating between the divine and the humans who call on him. His role is assisting humans and communicating divine messages to us. This chapter aims to explore the origins and characteristics of Archangel Uriel.

The knowledge in this chapter will open your eyes to a world beyond ours and give you a glance into a spiritual place in a deeper and more meaningful way. This chapter will introduce Uriel and explain what an archangel is. It will also explore the etymology of Uriel's name, his role in mysticism, his celestial role, and his close connection to the earthly realm. Lastly, this chapter will conclude by summarizing Uriel's key characteristics and roles in Heaven and on Earth. By the end of this chapter, you will better understand Uriel's place in the celestial realms.

An Introduction to Archangel Uriel

Archangel Uriel first appeared as the angel of wisdom and light in Abrahamic literature. He is one of the seven archangels who stand on the throne of God. Archangel Uriel is also associated with creativity, ideas, and judgment. He is often depicted holding a scroll in his hand, symbolizing knowledge, understanding, and wisdom. If you are seeking inspiration or guidance in your life, calling on Archangel Uriel may be just what you need. With his powerful presence and unwavering commitment to justice and truth, Archangel Uriel exists to help you navigate life's challenges and find your way toward enlightenment.

What Is an Archangel?

Angels are divine beings that play different roles in the spiritual world, but not all angels are created equal. Archangels are known to hold the highest rank in the angelic world and are believed to be powerful and influential beings. Archangels have been mentioned in several religious texts, including Christianity, Judaism, and Islam. This section will explore what an archangel is, its role in the angelic hierarchy system, and its significance in the angelic kingdom.

The Angelic Kingdom

The angelic kingdom is a realm that exists beyond our physical world but can often interact with us. It is a world where divine beings reside, and they are responsible for carrying out different duties. According to most religious texts, the angels were created by God, each having his own role, but they are primarily considered guardians and messengers. The angels' role in the angelic kingdom also includes protecting and guiding humanity, so they work closely with humans to ensure the divine plan is executed.

The Angelic Hierarchy System

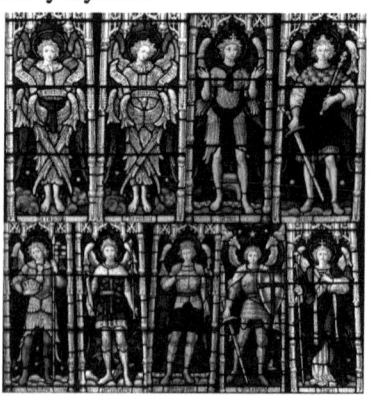

Angelic hierarchy.

Andrewrabbott, CC BY-SA 4.0 <https://creativecommons.org/licenses/by-sa/4.0>, via Wikimedia Commons: https://commons.wikimedia.org/wiki/File:Angelic_Hierarchy_in_Christianity,_St_Michael_and_All_Angels%27,_Somerton.jpg

In the angelic hierarchy system, archangels hold the highest rank. This means they have more power and influence than other angelic beings. They are known to be closest to God, and their purpose is to carry out God's divine will. However, there are different levels of angels, and archangels are just a part of the angelic hierarchy system.

The Divine Archangels

An archangel is a high-ranking angelic being believed to have more power and influence than regular angels. There are several archangels, and they are often associated with specific qualities or attributes. For example, Archangel Michael is the protector, while Archangel Raphael is the healer. Archangel Gabriel is revered in the Christian faith as being the angel who appeared to a young Jewish girl, Mary, with the message that she would become the mother of Jesus.

The Role of Archangels

Archangels play an essential role in the angelic kingdom. They are responsible for carrying out specific tasks that ensure God's divine plan is executed. Archangels are also responsible for helping humans in their mundane life, providing comfort and guidance when needed. They can aid human beings in earthly matters, such as love, career decisions, health issues, and spiritual growth.

The Significance of Archangels

Archangels hold a significant place in various religious texts, myths, and legends. Their significance stems from their status as powerful divine beings that are known to protect and guide humanity and are part of many belief systems, including Christian, Jewish and Islamic religions. They are also considered guardians of virtues such as truth, love, compassion, and wisdom and work with humans to help them achieve spiritual enlightenment and fulfill their life purpose.

Archangels are divine beings that hold a significant place in the angelic kingdom due to their power, influence, and relationship with God. Understanding the role of archangels can give us a better insight into the spiritual realm and help us connect with our spiritual side.

The Etymology of "Uriel" and His Origins

In the world of angels, Archangel Uriel is one of the most fascinating and enigmatic characters. He is associated with wisdom, illumination, and divine light. But where did Uriel come from? What does his name mean? This section will explore the etymology of the name Uriel and the origins of this intriguing archangel.

Meaning

To begin, let's look at the name "Uriel." In Hebrew, "Uriel" means "God is my light." This name is fitting for the archangel, who is the carrier of illumination and divine light. Interestingly, his name is also sometimes spelled "Auriel," and in some medieval texts, it is even spelled "Oriel." Regardless of the spelling, Uriel's name stands for radiance and divine guidance.

Origins

As for Uriel's origins, he is mentioned in several religious texts, including the Torah, the Bible, the Quran, and the Book of Enoch. In Jewish tradition, Uriel is one of the four primary archangels, along with Michael, Gabriel, and Raphael. In Christian tradition, Uriel is considered an archangel, though he is not mentioned in the canonical Bible.

Depictions

Uriel is often depicted as a wise and benevolent angel, offering guidance and illumination to those who seek it. Some stories even credit him as being the angel who warned Noah of the impending flood. He is also said to communicate divine messages to humankind, facilitating spiritual growth and understanding.

Art and Literature

One of the most fascinating aspects of Uriel is the way he is depicted in art and literature. He is shown holding a book in many works, illustrating his role as the angel of wisdom. He is often shown with a flame or a torch, signifying his association with divine light. In some texts, Uriel is even depicted as a warrior battling against evil forces. In modern times, Uriel is still revered by many and has become associated with various New Age beliefs and practices. Some people believe that Uriel can assist with emotional healing and personal transformation and seek his guidance through meditation, prayer, or even angel card readings.

Uriel is a fascinating and influential archangel. His name, which means "God is my light," perfectly represents his role as the carrier of divine guidance and illumination. Though his origins are somewhat mysterious, Uriel is considered a powerful force for good and has been revered by many throughout history. Whether you seek his guidance for spiritual growth or simply appreciate his significance in religious traditions, this enigmatic angel is sure to inspire awe and wonder.

Uriel's Identity According to Mysticism

Mysticism is a philosophy that embraces a vast range of beliefs, practices, and experiences to attain unity with the divine. One of the most intriguing concepts in the realm of mysticism is the angel Uriel. Over the years, Uriel has been the focus of several texts, including the Book of Enoch, the Biblical Apocrypha, and the Apocalypse of Peter, which have all sought to unveil Uriel's true identity. Let's explore these texts and unravel the mystery surrounding Uriel's identity according to mysticism.

Book of Enoch

The Book of Enoch is an ancient Jewish text that narrates the story of Enoch, the great-grandfather of Noah. In chapter XXI of the book, Uriel is described as one of the four archangels created by God. Uriel is said to have been entrusted with the universe's secrets, including the mysteries of the moon and the stars. In addition, Uriel is described as the angel who watches over thunder and terror, making him an angel of judgment. According to the Book of Enoch, Uriel's identity as an archangel makes him one of the highest-ranking angels in heaven.

Biblical Apocrypha

The Biblical Apocrypha also mentions Uriel as an archangel, although with a few variations. In 2 Esdras 4:1, Uriel is described as the angel who has been asked to interpret the vision given to Ezra, a Jewish prophet. Uriel is also called the "angel of repentance," implying his role as an angel of judgment. Nonetheless, Uriel's identity as an archangel remains consistent with the Book of Enoch.

Apocalypse of Peter

A third text that explores Uriel's identity is the Apocalypse of Peter, which is believed to have been written around the third century. In the text, Uriel is not explicitly mentioned but is described as the angel who stands at the gate of heaven, preventing sinners from entering the kingdom of God. This portrayal of Uriel is consistent with his role as an angel of judgment.

These three texts uncover Uriel's identity as an archangel with the power to interpret divine mysteries and exercise judgment. He is a messenger of God, entrusted with secrets known only to Him. Uriel is known as an angel of repentance and an enforcer of divine justice, making him a formidable figure in mysticism.

The mystery surrounding Uriel's identity is answered to a degree in the Book of Enoch, the Biblical Apocrypha, and the Apocalypse of Peter, which all confirm him as a being of divine authority and wisdom. Uriel is a source of fascination and respect in the world of mysticism and remains an enigmatic figure to this day.

Exploring Archangel Uriel's Celestial Role

From ancient times, people have believed in the existence of heavenly beings, archangels, and angels, who are imbued with immense power and divine grace. Uriel is associated with light or fire; some have even revered him as an Angel of Judgment. In this section, we will explore his celestial role and dive into the subtle yet powerful ways in which Uriel guides souls through their life journey.

The Bringer of Light and Wisdom

This divine being is known for shedding light on people's paths, illuminating their minds, and bringing clarity to their thoughts. Uriel is also considered the patron saint of science and education, as he is believed to inspire new ideas and facilitate learning.

The Angel of Repentance and Forgiveness

As the angel of repentance and forgiveness, Uriel is often called upon to help people let go of their past mistakes and find redemption. Uriel is believed to have the power to cleanse people's hearts, guide them toward righteousness, and inspire them to seek forgiveness from the divine. Many people pray to Uriel in times of turmoil, seeking his guidance and grace.

The Protector and Guardian

Archangel Uriel is also said to watch over the gates of the underworld, protecting the souls from harm and defending the realm of the divine. Uriel is believed to work closely with other celestial beings, such as Michael and Gabriel, to protect the realm of the divine from any threats or negative energies.

The Divine Strategist

As the patron saint of science and education, Uriel is often associated with strategic thinking and long-term planning. Uriel is believed to inspire people to think deeply about their decisions, weigh the pros and cons, and consider the long-term impact of their actions. Many people pray to Uriel for guidance during moments of decision-making, seeking his support and wisdom.

The Angel of Earth and Nature

Finally, Uriel is also revered as the angel of earth and nature. This celestial being is believed to have a deep connection with the earth, and he can communicate with the spirits of nature. Uriel is believed to help people understand the natural world around them, connect with the healing energies of nature, and develop a deep reverence for all living beings.

Archangel Uriel is a powerful yet subtle celestial being who is key in guiding souls through their life journey. As the bringer of light and wisdom, the angel of repentance and forgiveness, the protector and guardian, the divine strategist, and the angel of earth and nature, Uriel holds immense power and grace. Many people worldwide pray to Uriel for guidance, support, and wisdom, believing he holds the key to unlocking their deepest potential and leading them toward righteousness. As we explore Uriel's celestial role, let us open our hearts and minds to the divine grace he generously offers.

Archangel Uriel's Epithets and Attributes

As we strive to understand the infinite and the divine, exploring the essence and characteristics of each archangel is a powerful tool. As the highest-ranking angels, these archangels have been entrusted with particular duties and attributes to help guide us through life's obstacles. Archangel Uriel is one of the most beloved archangels, known for his wisdom, illuminating light, and spiritual guidance. This section will explore Archangel Uriel's epithets and attributes that help us connect with him for personal growth and healing.

Epithets are descriptive terms often accompanying an archangel's name that describes his role or symbolism. Archangel Uriel is also known as the light of God, the angel of wisdom, and the prince of light. His name means the "fire of God" because he embodies divine justice and the sacred fire that purifies the soul. Uriel's attributes are visual symbols representing him, and each symbolizes part of his divine qualities, like his light or wisdom. Here are some of the most commonly used epithets and attributes of Archangel Uriel.

- **Light:** One of Uriel's most significant attributes is light. His light represents the divine illumination of knowledge and understanding. It is said that His light can assist us in awakening our inner light and growing spiritually.
- **Scroll:** Uriel is often depicted holding a scroll representing divine knowledge and wisdom. He is the guardian of the Book of Knowledge and holds the secrets of spiritual enlightenment.
- **Sun:** The sun is not only a symbol of light but also of power and energy. Uriel's association with the sun represents his powers that provide us with the vital energy of life.
- **Sword:** The sword commonly represents strength, force, and power. As Archangel Uriel is responsible for divine justice, the sword symbolizes his role in protecting and upholding the law.
- **Flame**: Archangel Uriel's flame symbol is one of the most potent symbols in his iconography. The flame represents the purification, illumination, and transformation of our souls.

Archangel Uriel's epithets and attributes signify divine qualities such as wisdom, knowledge, divine light, and justice. Each name and attribute conveys different aspects of his nature and meaning, allowing us to understand and connect with him more profoundly. He is also considered the patron of the arts, channeling intuition and insight and promoting healing and harmony between people. To connect with Archangel Uriel, you can use his visual attributes, recite his prayers, or create a sacred space to meditate and connect with him. Knowing his epithets and attributes helps us feel closer to his protective and guiding presence, initiating a path toward personal growth, healing, and spiritual enlightenment.

Uriel's Close Connection to the Earthly Realm

When it comes to archangels, there is perhaps no other angel more closely linked with the earthly realm than Archangel Uriel. As the angel of wisdom, he is said to preside over the Earth and its elements. His presence is believed to be felt in forests, mountains, and rivers as he watches over the natural world. This section will delve deeper into the significance of Archangel Uriel's connection to the earthly realm and how different cultures worldwide worship him.

The Angel of Wisdom

Archangel Uriel's connection to the earthly realm is rooted in his status as the angel of wisdom. Wisdom is often linked to knowledge of the natural world and the environment around us, so it is no surprise that he is closely associated with the Earth. His name means "God is my light," and he is believed to provide humans with knowledge and understanding of the world and our place in it.

Patron Saint of the Natural World

In many cultures, Archangel Uriel is worshiped as the patron saint of the natural world. In Native American traditions, he is associated with the seasons and the changing of the Earth. In Celtic cultures, he is connected to the elements of air and earth, and in Hinduism, he is worshiped as a teacher of knowledge and wisdom. His influence spans many different cultures and beliefs.

Association with Autumnal Equinox

Another aspect of Archangel Uriel's connection to the earthly realm is his association with the autumnal equinox. This is when day and night are equal in length, and it is believed that Archangel Uriel oversees this transition. He is said to be most present and receptive to worshipers seeking his guidance on this day.

Protector of Humans

In addition to overseeing the natural world, Archangel Uriel is also believed to be a protector of humans. He is called on in times of trouble or despair, as his wisdom and guidance can help us find our way through difficult times. His connection to the earthly realm also means he is closely attuned to human suffering and can offer comfort and strength when needed most.

Archangel Uriel's connection to the earthly realm highlights the importance of respecting and protecting the natural world around us. His role as the angel of wisdom means that he can offer guidance and insight into the environment and all the elements it contains. His influence spans many cultures and traditions, and his association with the autumnal equinox underscores his importance as a protector and guide. Whether seeking guidance in times of trouble or looking to deepen our understanding of the world around us, Archangel Uriel remains a powerful force for good in the world.

Archangel Uriel is also known for his incredible intellect and wisdom. As one of the four archangels, his role in heaven is to assist God in carrying out his divine plan, and he is often referred to as the "light of God" due to his immense knowledge and understanding of the universe. On earth, Archangel Uriel is known for his ability to provide insight and inspiration, helping them see the bigger picture and find meaning in their lives. With his cheerful personality and positive energy, Archangel Uriel is an uplifting presence wherever he goes, always ready to offer guidance and support to those in need. If you are looking for a source of wisdom and inspiration, look no further than this incredible archangel!

Chapter 2: Invoking Archangel Uriel

Invoking Archangel Uriel is an amazing experience that can clear your mind, uplift your spirits, and connect you with the divine. Uriel, known as the angel of wisdom and enlightenment, can bless you with a deeper understanding of yourself and the world around you when you are in his presence. You can call on him for guidance, support, and protection; he will always assist you with your journey. Whether you are facing a difficult challenge or just want to feel more connected to the universe, invoking Archangel Uriel is a powerful way to tap into your inner power and unleash your full potential.

Archangel Uriel, the angel of wisdom.
https://commons.wikimedia.org/wiki/File:Image_of_Uriel_the_Archangel,_Cairo.jpg

This chapter will provide an in-depth look at how to successfully invoke Archangel Uriel. It will start by defining the term "invoke" and explain how it works when attempting a connection with angelic figures. It will also discuss the importance of intention and receptiveness in this process and provide several step-by-step exercises, meditations, affirmations, and mantras to help communicate with him. Suggestions for daily exercises that will help develop the ability to sense an angelic presence will be provided as bonus content here.

Definition of Invocation

When invoking something, many different images may come to mind. Some may think of summoning a powerful being from another realm, while others may picture prayer or blessings. In essence, an invocation is an act of calling upon a higher power, whether that be a deity, a force of nature, or even the collective energy of a group of individuals. While the specific practices may vary greatly depending on culture, religion, or belief systems, the underlying idea is universal. By invoking something greater than ourselves, we have access to more power, wisdom, or guidance than we could on our own. So, whether you are a believer or a skeptic, the concept of invocation is something worth exploring and contemplating. Who knows? You may just tap into something truly transformative.

Unraveling the Mysteries Behind Invocation

Invocation as a concept has been around for hundreds of years, but to most people, it remains a mystery. It is a powerful way of calling or praying to a higher being who can unlock the immense potential within us and help us achieve our goals. If you have ever wondered how invocation works, you have come to the right place. This section will explore this fascinating concept and show how it can help you reach your full potential.

At its core, invocation is all about connecting with a higher power. This can be a religious figure or simply an abstract concept like the universe. The idea is that when you can connect with this higher power, you are tapping into a source of energy and strength that you would not ordinarily have access to. This can help you achieve things you might have otherwise considered impossible.

The process of invocation is relatively straightforward. It involves creating a sacred space and performing a ritual of some sort. This can be as simple as lighting a candle and meditating or as complex as performing an elaborate ceremony. The purpose of the ritual is to create a sense of reverence and respect for the higher power you are invoking.

One important thing to remember when undertaking an invocation is that you are not simply asking for a favor. Rather, you are creating a connection and forming a relationship with the higher power you are invoking. This means you must be prepared to give something of yourself in return. This could be as simple as expressing gratitude or as complex as making a sacrifice.

The benefits of invocation are many. For one thing, it can help you overcome fear and self-doubt. When you feel connected to a higher power, you are more likely to feel empowered and capable of achieving your goals. Your invocation can also help you feel a sense of purpose and direction. You will likely stay motivated and focused when you have a clear idea of what you want to achieve.

Whether pursuing a personal goal or seeking spiritual growth, invoking a higher power gives you the boost you need to reach your objectives. By creating a sacred space, performing a ritual, and developing a relationship with the higher power you are invoking, you can unlock immense strength and potential within yourself. So, if you have ever wondered how invocation works, why not give it a try? Who knows what wonders you might achieve?

The Role of Intention and Receptiveness

Have you ever felt a presence around you, but you couldn't put your finger on what or who it was? Many people believe angelic figures surround us every day. Whether you believe in angels or not, something is to be said about the peaceful and uplifting energy surrounding us when we feel connected to these divine beings. The key to invoking angelic figures is through intention and receptiveness. Let's explore the power of intention and receptiveness in invoking angelic figures.

Intention

The first key to invoking angelic figures is intention. Many people pray or meditate with a specific intention, such as guidance, healing, or protection. When you set an intention, you invite angelic figures to align with you and help you reach your goal. A simple way to set your intention is to focus on what you wish to accomplish and then ask your guardian angels or other divine figures for assistance. A clear intention is the first step in creating a strong connection with your guardian angels.

Receptiveness

The second key to invoking angelic figures is receptiveness. When you are receptive, you are open to receiving guidance and support from the universe. This means that you must be open to receiving messages from your angels, even if they come in unconventional ways. Angelic figures may communicate with you through symbols or signs, like seeing the same number repeatedly or noticing a certain flower blooming at a specific time. By remaining open and receptive, you allow yourself to receive guidance and support from your angels in a way that works best for you.

Trust

The third key to invoking angelic figures is trust. Trusting that your angels are always there to guide and protect you can make a huge difference in how you perceive the world around you. By trusting that your angels are working behind the scenes to help you, you can release any fear, worry, or anxiety you may be experiencing. This trust gives you inner peace and serenity that can help you stay grounded and centered in your daily life.

Gratitude

The fourth and final key to invoking angelic figures is gratitude. When you are grateful for the blessings that come your way, both big and small, you open yourself up to receiving even more abundance from the universe. Expressing gratitude for the guidance and support you receive from your angels will help you create a deeper sense of connection with them. Gratitude can also help you shift your focus away from negative thoughts and emotions and instead focus on the positive aspects of your life.

Invoking angelic figures is all about intention, receptiveness, trust, and gratitude. You can create a stronger connection with your angels by setting a clear intention and remaining open and receptive. Trusting that your angels are always there to guide and protect you can help you release fear and worry while expressing gratitude for their help can create a deeper sense of connection. Whether you believe in angels or not, these tips can help you align with the positive energy surrounding you daily.

When Can Archangel Uriel Help?

Archangel Uriel is one of the four main archangels in many spiritual traditions. He represents wisdom, knowledge, and illumination and is often called upon to bring clarity and understanding to difficult situations. Uriel is also known as the *archangel of salvation*, helping individuals and entire communities overcome difficulties and find hope in the most trying times. So, when can Archangel Uriel help you?

Feeling Lost or Unsure of Your Path

When you're feeling lost or uncertain about which path to take to move forward, Archangel Uriel will come to help you. If you are facing a difficult decision about your career, a relationship, or any other area of life, Uriel provides the clarity and guidance you need. By calling upon Uriel, you can connect with your inner wisdom and develop a deeper understanding of your purpose and what steps you need to take to achieve your goals.

Struggling with a Difficult Situation

If you are going through a challenging time, such as a health crisis, financial difficulty, or personal loss, Archangel Uriel will be the one to comfort and support you. He can help you to find peace and hope amid even the most challenging circumstances. You can tap into his divine energy and draw strength from his wisdom and guidance by asking Uriel for assistance.

Feeling Overwhelmed or Stressed

Archangel Uriel can also help when you feel overwhelmed, stressed, or anxious. His presence can bring a sense of calm and peace, helping you to let go of worries and fears and focus on the present. By connecting with Uriel, you can find the strength to face any challenge with grace and ease.

Seeking to Deepen Your Spiritual Connection

Archangel Uriel can be an invaluable guide and mentor for those seeking a greater connection with the divine. He can help you to deepen your spiritual practice, expand your awareness, and connect deeper with your inner wisdom. By working with Uriel, you can build a stronger relationship with the divine and open yourself up to new levels of insight and understanding.

Looking to Heal and Transform

Finally, Archangel Uriel can help when you want to heal and transform on all levels. Whether you are dealing with physical, emotional, or spiritual challenges, Uriel can help you to release negative patterns, beliefs, and emotions and move into a more positive, joyful state of being. By working with Uriel, you can help to transform your life and step into a place of greater love, light, and healing.

Archangel Uriel is a powerful and compassionate ally for anyone needing to overcome challenges, deepen their spiritual connection, and live a more fulfilling life. Whether facing difficult circumstances, seeking greater clarity and understanding, or looking to heal and transform on all levels, Uriel is there to guide and support you. So, if you need his help, simply call on him with an open heart and mind, and trust that he will be there to assist you every step of the way.

Step-by-Step Exercises to Connect with Archangel Uriel

Do you ever feel you need help, guidance, or support from the heavenly realm? Archangels are known to provide just that, especially Archangel Uriel. He is the angel of wisdom, knowledge, and insight, and he can definitely come to your aid. This section will set out three step-by-step exercises to connect with Archangel Uriel: meditations, affirmations, and mantras.

Exercise 1: Meditation

Meditation is a powerful skill to use to connect with the divine. To begin, find a quiet and peaceful space to sit comfortably. Close your eyes and take a few deep breaths. Visualize yourself surrounded by a golden light, protecting you and guiding you. Then, visualize Archangel Uriel standing before you, radiating wisdom and knowledge. Ask him for guidance or clarity on a particular situation, and listen to his response. You may receive messages through thoughts, feelings, or even physical sensations. Finish the meditation by thanking Archangel Uriel for his guidance.

Exercise 2: Affirmations

Affirmations are positive statements that reprogram your subconscious mind. To connect with Archangel Uriel using affirmations, try repeating the following statements each day:

- Archangel Uriel, please guide me toward the path of wisdom and knowledge.
- I am open to receiving guidance and insight from Archangel Uriel.
- Archangel Uriel, please bless me with clarity and understanding in all areas of my life.

Repeat these affirmations in the morning or before bed, or whenever you need extra support.

Exercise 3: Mantras

Mantras are sacred words or phrases that are repeated to create a sense of peace, calm, and harmony. To connect with Archangel Uriel using mantras, try chanting the following at least 108 times:

- Om Anandamayi Namah (I am filled with divine joy)
- Divyatma Prabhu Pragaya Namah (God's light is within me and around me)

Chanting these mantras will unlock your inner wisdom, and you will be receptive to guidance from Archangel Uriel. They invoke Archangel Uriel's energy and clear your mind and bring focus to your thoughts. Repeat the mantra while sitting in a calm, peaceful environment, and visualize Archangel Uriel's energy surrounding you. Using these three exercises, you can deepen your connection with Archangel Uriel and receive his guidance and support whenever needed. Remember to trust the process and have faith that you will receive the necessary messages.

Developing the Ability to Sense an Angelic Presence

Have you ever felt a presence that you couldn't quite explain? Or perhaps you've had an experience that left you feeling uplifted and inspired, even though you couldn't quite put your finger on why. Perhaps you were sensing the presence of an angelic being. Angels are believed to be spiritual beings who exist to help guide and protect us on our journey through life. However, not everyone can sense their presence. This section will explore some techniques to help you develop your ability to sense an angelic presence.

Cultivate a State of Receptivity

One of the keys to sensing the presence of angels is cultivating a state of receptivity. This means opening yourself to subtle sensations and impressions you might normally overlook. To do this, try practicing mindfulness meditation, which involves bringing your attention to the sensations of your body and the present moment. As you become more attuned to your physical and emotional experiences, you may also sense the presence of spiritual beings.

Pay Attention to Your Intuition

Another way to sense the presence of angels is to pay attention to your intuition. Intuition is often described as a "gut feeling" or a sense of knowing that comes from beyond the rational mind. Many people believe that angels communicate with us through our intuition, so it's necessary to develop this faculty. To do this, try journaling about your intuitive hunches and paying attention to any synchronicities or coincidences that occur in your life.

Practice Gratitude

Gratitude is a powerful tool for attracting positive energy and spiritual connections. When we cultivate a sense of gratefulness for the blessings in our lives, we open ourselves up to receiving even more blessings. To practice gratitude, try keeping a gratitude journal where you write down three things you're grateful for daily. You can also make a gratitude altar where you place items that represent things you're thankful for and spend a few moments each day reflecting on them.

Ask for Assistance

Angels are always willing to assist us but won't intervene unless we ask for their help. If you're struggling with a problem or need guidance, try asking your angels for assistance. You can do this through prayer, meditation, or simply speaking aloud as if you're talking to a trusted friend. Be specific about what you need help with, and trust that your angels will come to your aid.

Trust Your Experience

Finally, trust your experience when you sense the presence of angels. Some people may dismiss your experiences as "just your imagination" or "wishful thinking," but only you can know what you sense and feel. Trust that your experiences are valid, even if you can't prove them to others.

Developing your ability to sense the presence of angels can be a powerful ability for navigating life's challenges and connecting with the divine. By cultivating a state of receptivity, paying attention to your intuition, practicing gratitude, asking for assistance, and trusting your experiences, you can become more and more attuned to the subtle energies and spiritual guidance surrounding us all. With time and practice, you may find that you can sense the presence of angels more readily and that your interactions with them bring peace, comfort, and inspiration to your life.

Daily Exercises

Angels are often regarded as celestial beings here to help and protect us. They are said to bring us guidance, inspiration, and support in times of need. While some people may find it easier to sense the presence of angels than others, there are ways to develop your ability to sense them. Here are some daily exercises that can help you to sense an angelic presence.

- **Nature Walks:** Nature is a wonderful way to connect with the energy of angels. Take a walk in nature every day and pay attention to the signs around you. Notice the birds, the trees, the flowers, the wind, and other elements of nature. Be open to receiving messages from your angels through these signs. You may also ask your angels to join you on your walk and guide you along your path.
- **Journaling:** Journaling is an excellent way to connect with the energy of angels and receive their guidance. Write down your thoughts and feelings daily, and invite your angels to communicate with you through your writing. You may also write down any signs or messages you receive from your angels throughout the day.
- **Yoga and Meditation:** Yoga and meditation are both great methods to connect with the energy of angels. Spend some time each day practicing yoga or meditating, and focus on the intention of opening yourself up to the presence of angelic beings. As you practice, ask your angels to join you and provide guidance.

By incorporating these daily exercises into your routine, you can develop your ability to sense an angelic presence. Remember to stay open, receptive, and trusting, and allow the energy of angels to surround you. With practice, you will become more confident in your ability to sense their presence and receive their guidance. Trust that your angels are always with you, guiding you toward your highest good.

Invoking archangels can be a powerful way to connect with the divine and receive guidance. By cultivating a state of receptivity, paying attention to your intuition, practicing gratitude, asking for assistance, and trusting your experiences, you can become more attuned to the subtle energies of these angelic presences. With time and practice, developing a deeper relationship with your angels and accessing their wisdom is possible. Remember to stay open, trusting, and receptive as you explore this realm of spiritual connection. Your angels are here for you, so don't be afraid to seek help when needed. Your journey toward a deeper understanding of angelic guidance will surely bring peace, comfort, and inspiration into your life.

Chapter 3: Signs of Uriel's Presence

Uriel is the Archangel of Wisdom and a messenger between God and people. He delivers his messages to us through signs, symbols, and omens. Although Uriel is known to communicate through various means, his presence can be recognized by certain symbols and signs. To understand better what these signs and symbols are and what they mean, we need a clear understanding of Uriel's role in our lives.

This chapter will provide a general overview of the symbols and signs associated with Uriel's presence while exploring in depth the various aspects of Uriel's role as an Archangel of Wisdom. It'll also look into the personal experiences of people who have come in contact with Uriel and how this practice has affected their perception of life. By the end of the chapter, you should better understand the signs and symbols that indicate Uriel's presence.

Unraveling the Meanings of the Symbols and Depictions of Uriel

Uriel is one of the archangels mentioned in the Jewish, Christian, and Islamic holy books. He is often called the light of God, and his name translates to "God is my light." Over the years, various symbols and depictions of Uriel have emerged, each carrying a unique meaning. This section will take a closer look at some of these symbols and what they

signify.
The Flame

Uriel is commonly depicted holding a flaming torch.
https://www.pexels.com/photo/orange-flame-635926/

The first symbol associated with Uriel is the flame. Uriel holds a flaming torch or sits atop a fiery orb in many illustrations. This flame signifies the light part of his name, *light of God*. The light radiates from him, bringing clarity and illumination to the world. The flame also represents Uriel's passion for aiding humanity in finding its way back to God's divine light.

The Book

Another symbol that is commonly associated with Uriel is a book. In Christian illustrations, he is often depicted carrying an open book or a scroll, representing knowledge given to him by God. The book also symbolizes Uriel's role as a divine teacher, offering enlightenment to those open to it. As the angel of wisdom, Uriel is thought to guide individuals to the truth of God's plan for humanity.

The Scales

The third symbol is the scales. The scales of justice are also associated with Uriel, symbolizing his role as a divine judge. The scales represent the balance and fairness that Uriel is said to bring when passing judgment, ensuring that each decision he makes is just and fair. Those feeling lost or overwhelmed often turn to the energy of Uriel to bring balance to their lives.

Bow and Arrow

Finally, Uriel is often shown holding a bow and arrow. These symbols represent his role in helping people conquer their fears and anxieties. Uriel's energy is said to inspire courage and bravery, the characteristics we need when facing challenging situations. He is also thought to help us tap into our inner strength and stand our ground in the face of adversity.

When we look at these symbols and depictions of Uriel, we see an archangel who represents the light, knowledge, fairness, and courage of God. Uriel's energy can help us find our way back to our true purpose and bring clarity to our lives. By understanding these symbols, we can tap into his energy and allow him to guide us toward finding our true selves. So let us embrace the light of Uriel and allow his energy to guide us toward wisdom, justice, and courage in our lives.

Repetitive Numbers: Signs of Uriel's Presence

Have you ever experienced seeing the same numbers over and over again? Perhaps, you glanced at the clock, and it was 11:11, then later on, you noticed the same numbers on your phone and computer screen? Believe it or not, this could be a sign that Archangel Uriel is trying to communicate with you. Let's dive into repetitive numbers and how it relates to Uriel's presence.

Angel Numbers

Since Uriel is associated with wisdom, he often communicates with us through signs and symbols, including repetitive numbers. Seeing repetitive numbers is a common sign from Uriel, and it is often referred to as "angel numbers" or "divine messages." Each number has a meaning and significance, and paying attention to the numbers shown to you is important. For instance, seeing the number 1111 can represent new beginnings and spiritual awakening. Meanwhile, the number 333 can symbolize growth and progress.

It's not just the individual numbers that are significant but also the *repetition of the numbers*. The more you see the same number repeated, the stronger the message from Uriel is. So, if you keep seeing the number 777, this could suggest that Uriel is acknowledging your spiritual progress and achievement.

Deciphering the Messages

There are a few ways to decipher the messages from Uriel through repetitive numbers. Firstly, take note and remember the numbers that you keep seeing. You can research the meanings of these numbers online or through spiritual guides to understand what they signify. Another approach is to ask a question in your mind, then pay attention to the next set of numbers you see after posing the question. The number could hold the answer to your query.

Seeing repetitive numbers doesn't necessarily have to be a spiritual experience. It could simply be your mind attuning itself to patterns. However, if you do believe in the spiritual significance of seeing repetitive numbers, take the time to appreciate the message being sent to you.

Seeing repetitive numbers indicates that Uriel is trying to communicate with you. Pay attention to the numbers shown to you and their repetition. Take note of the numbers you see and their meanings, and try to understand Uriel's message. Whether it's a message of reassurance or guidance, Uriel's presence can provide a sense of comfort and understanding. So, the next time you see repetitive numbers, take a moment to appreciate the message being sent to you.

Animal Encounters: Signs of Uriel's Presence

When it comes to experiencing the divine, there are many ways to do so. Some of us may meditate and feel a sense of calm or hear a voice inside our heads. Others may feel the presence of someone or something watching over them. For those who believe in the existence of angels, animal encounters can be a clear sign of their presence. Uriel, the archangel of wisdom, is known to communicate using animals to send his messages to people. Here are different signs of Uriel's presence through animal encounters.

- **Birds:** If you look up to the sky and notice a bird circling you, it could be a sign of Uriel's presence. According to spiritual beliefs, birds are messengers of the angelic realm. When you see a bird, watch its behavior. Does it seem to be trying to catch your attention? Does it fly close to you? These could be signs that Uriel is trying to communicate with you, reminding you to trust in your intuition and spiritual path

- **Butterflies**: Butterflies are symbols of transformation and change. If a butterfly lands on you or follows you wherever you go, it could be a sign from Uriel that you need to make some changes in your life. Butterflies can also signify a spiritual awakening, urging you to pursue your passion and purpose in life
- **Owls**: It is said that Uriel often communicates with people through owls. Owls are symbols of wisdom, intuition, and transformation. If you regularly see owls at night or during meditation, Uriel may be guiding you toward a deeper understanding of yourself and the world around you
- **Dogs:** Dogs are known for their loyalty and unconditional love. If you have a dog, pay attention to its behavior. Does it seem to be trying to tell you something? Does it behave differently when you are feeling sad or anxious? Dogs can sense our emotions and may be trying to comfort us or remind us to be kind to ourselves
- **Cats:** Cats are independent animals that seem to have a sixth sense when it comes to energy. If you have a cat, observe its behavior. Does it seem to be attracted to certain people or places? Does it seem to be picking up on negative energy in the house? Cats can help us tune into our intuition and remind us to trust our instincts

Animal encounters can be a sign of Uriel's presence in our lives. Whether it's a bird, a butterfly, an owl, a dog, or a cat, these creatures can communicate with us in ways we may not even realize. By paying attention to their behavior and symbolism, we can receive spiritual guidance from the angelic realm, reminding us to trust in our intuition, pursue our passions, and spread love and kindness wherever we go.

Instincts: Signs of Uriel's Presence

When we feel lost, alone, or unsure of ourselves, we often find comfort in spirituality. We look for guidance and seek the answers to our questions. It can be very comforting to believe that someone is guiding us and watching over us. For many people, that guiding force is Uriel.

Uriel brings answers, insight, and healing into our lives. But how can we know if Uriel is present with us or if it's something else? By learning to recognize the signs of his presence in our lives, we can deepen our connection to him and find more guidance and support.

This section will explore the instincts often associated with Uriel's presence. From intuitive feelings to physical sensations, these signs can help us to feel more connected to Uriel and our higher power and more confident in our spiritual journey.

A Feeling of Warmth and Comfort

When Uriel is present, many people have reported feeling a sense of warmth and comfort. It can feel like being wrapped in a cozy blanket or sitting by a crackling fire. This sensation can occur at any time, but it's often most noticeable when we're feeling lost, scared, or uncertain. If you find yourself suddenly feeling warm and comforted, take a moment to recognize Uriel's presence in your life.

Sudden Insights and Clarity

Uriel is the archangel of wisdom, so it's no surprise that his presence often brings clarity and insight. You may suddenly have a flash of inspiration, a new understanding of a problem, or a realization that helps you see things in a new light. These insights can come to us in many ways, from a sudden urge to write something down to a feeling of certainty about a decision. Pay attention to these moments and see if you can recognize Uriel's hand in them.

A Feeling of Protection

Uriel is also known for his protective energy; many people report feeling safer and more secure when he's near. You may notice that you're less prone to accidents, feel more confident in your abilities, or are more aware of your surroundings. This protective energy can be very comforting, especially during times of difficulty or danger.

A Sense of Peace and Calm

When Uriel is present, many people report feeling a sense of peace and calm. This can be especially helpful during times of stress, anxiety, or worry. You may suddenly feel more centered, more grounded, clearer-headed, or more at ease. This sense of peace can help you to focus on what's important and let go of distractions and worries.

An Intuitive Feeling

Finally, Uriel's presence is often accompanied by a strong intuitive feeling. You may suddenly feel as if you know what to do or have a sense of what's going to happen next. This kind of intuition can be very powerful and can guide you through difficult or confusing situations. If you ever have a strong intuitive feeling, take a moment to consider whether Uriel might be trying to communicate with you.

Uriel's presence can bring comfort, clarity, protection, peace, and intuitive guidance into our lives. By learning to recognize the signs of his presence, we can deepen our connection to this powerful archangel and find more guidance and support along our spiritual journey. Whether you feel a sudden warmth, gain new insights, or just feel a sense of peace, take a moment to acknowledge Uriel's presence in your life and let it guide you toward greater wisdom and light.

Sudden Flashes of Inspiration: Signs of Uriel's Presence

We all know that feeling of sudden inspiration that strikes us out of nowhere. It's that moment when our minds are suddenly filled with an idea, a solution to a problem we've been struggling with, or a newfound sense of purpose. But where does this sudden inspiration come from? Could it be that the archangel Uriel is trying to communicate with us? Here are some signs of Uriel's presence and what they could mean for you.

Dazzling Flashes of Light

One of the most common signs of Uriel's presence is a sudden flash of light, often accompanied by a tingling sensation. This could be a sign that Uriel is trying to guide you toward a new path or help you see things in a new light. Pay attention to any patterns or colors in the flashes of light, as they could hold clues about what Uriel is trying to communicate to you.

A Sense of Inner Peace

When Uriel is near, you may feel a sense of inner peace and serenity that radiates throughout your entire being. This is a sign that Uriel is gently guiding you toward a state of calmness and clarity so that you can receive the messages and insights coming your way with more assurance. If you're feeling overwhelmed or stuck in a rut, call on Uriel to help you find your way back to a state of peace and tranquility.

Synchronicities and Coincidences

Another sign that Uriel is trying to communicate with you is the appearance of synchronicities and coincidences in your life. This could be anything from repeatedly seeing the same numbers or symbols to running into people who share your passions or interests at unexpected times. These synchronicities are often little nudges from Uriel, urging you to pay attention and follow the breadcrumbs to uncover new opportunities or paths meant for you.

A Sense of Heightened Intuition

Uriel is known as the archangel of wisdom and intuition, so it's no surprise that his presence often leads to a heightened sense of intuition and inner knowing. You may find that you're suddenly more attuned to your thoughts and feelings and those of others around you. Trust these intuitive insights, as they could be invaluable in guiding you toward your true purpose or calling.

Inspiration Bursts and Creative Surges

Perhaps the most overt signs of Uriel's presence are the sudden bursts of inspiration and creative energy that come seemingly out of nowhere. You may feel a sudden urge to start a new project, write a book, or learn a new skill. These inspiration bursts are often gifts from Uriel, who is helping you tap into your creative potential and express it in ways that will serve you and others.

The signs of Uriel's presence are varied and nuanced. From flashes of light and inner peace to synchronicities and heightened intuition, Uriel constantly tries to communicate with us and guide us toward our highest good. The key is to remain open, receptive, and trusting of the signs and messages that come your way. Whether you're seeking a new path, a renewed sense of purpose, or simply a deeper connection to yourself and the universe, Uriel is always there, ready, and willing to help you find your way.

Finding Uriel's Presence through Electrical Signs

Known as the Angel of Light, Uriel is the archangel of wisdom and illumination. A lesser-known fact about Uriel is that he is also associated with electrical signs. This section will explore the signs of Uriel's presence and how to recognize them.

Electrical Surges

One of the most common signs believed to be associated with Uriel's presence is electrical surges. You might have experienced your lights flickering or the intensity of the sparkle in your light bulbs increasing.

Some people also believe that Uriel sometimes turns off electrical appliances or gadgets to grab your attention.

Feeling the Energy

Another way to recognize Uriel's presence is by paying attention to your energy levels. You might feel a sudden surge of energy or chill, indicating that Uriel is creating a pathway to communicate with you. It is said that during such moments, you might also receive visions or messages from Uriel telepathically or through intuition.

The Power of Numbers

Uriel is also associated with the numerical sequence of 111. If you start seeing 111 frequently or repeatedly, it is believed to be a sign of Uriel's presence. Seeing triple digits or repetitive numbers is also associated with the archangel of forgiveness, unity, and peace.

Unusual Events

Another sign of Uriel's presence is when you experience unusual events that defy your understanding of logic or science. It could be a coincidental meeting with someone familiar or discovering an object you have been searching for. These events might seem insignificant, but they could reveal Uriel's presence and protection to you.

Sensing a Presence

Lastly, you might sense Uriel's presence through your intuition or inner voice. Your gut feeling could signify that Uriel is with you, watching over and guiding you. Trusting this feeling and working on your intuitive abilities can help you connect with Uriel on a deeper level.

Uriel's electrical signs and presence might be challenging to recognize initially, but with time and patience, you will be able to connect with the Angel of Light. Always remember to stay positive, open, and curious about the world around you. Uriel's guidance and wisdom are there to help you navigate your life's purpose with greater clarity and ease. Keep your eyes open to electrical signs and trust the feeling of warmth and positivity that follows!

The Incredible Stories of Uriel's Presence

Millions of people around the world believe in the power of angels. These divine beings are known to bring comfort, protection, guidance, and support to those who believe in them. Among the archangels, Uriel is considered one of the most powerful and loving. Uriel is said to bring messages of hope, healing, and light to humanity. This section will explore the real accounts of personal experiences of Uriel's presence and what people have to say about his impact on their lives.

Healing through a Divine Vision

Many people have experienced some sort of physical, mental, or emotional healing through Uriel's presence. For example, there have been reports of people experiencing visions of Uriel during severe illness or emotional turmoil. These visions have brought comfort and healing, giving people the strength to endure and overcome their challenges. One woman shares that she saw Uriel during a time of deep sorrow and instantly felt a sense of peace and comfort. She believes that Uriel was sent to her as a messenger of hope, reminding her that she was loved and that everything would be OK.

Comfort in Times of Grief

Uriel is also known to help people cope with loss and grief. There have been numerous accounts of people feeling his presence after the death of a loved one. One woman shares that she was struggling to come to terms with the sudden death of her husband. One night, as she had trouble sleeping, she felt a strong presence in her room. She looked up to see Uriel standing there, holding out his hand. She felt an instant sense of peace and comfort, knowing that her husband was in good hands and that Uriel would help her through her grief.

Protection and Guidance

People have also reported feeling Uriel's presence when they were in danger or facing a difficult decision. Uriel is a powerful guardian angel, protecting those who believe in him from harm. One man shares that he was driving late at night on a deserted road when he felt his car suddenly stop. As he got out to check the engine, he felt a strong presence behind him. When he turned around, he saw Uriel standing there, with a look of reassurance on his face. The man felt a sudden sense of safety and knew that Uriel had stopped him to prevent him from being in a potentially dangerous situation.

Signs of Uriel's Presence

Many people have reported seeing signs of Uriel's presence, even if they didn't see him directly. Some people have seen rainbows or clouds in the shape of an angel or have felt a sudden breeze or temperature change. Uriel communicates through signs and symbols, letting people know he is with them and watching over them. One woman shared that she was struggling with a difficult decision and asked for Uriel's guidance.

Later that day, she saw a butterfly land on her hand and stay there for minutes. She knew that it was a sign from Uriel telling her to trust her instincts and make the right decision.

These stories of Uriel's presence are truly inspiring and uplifting. Uriel has a powerful impact on the lives of those who believe in him. Whether it is through healing, comfort, protection, or guidance, Uriel is a beacon of hope in a world that often seems dark and scary. So, if you ever feel lost, alone, or afraid, just remember that Uriel is always with you, watching over you and guiding you toward the light.

This chapter has explored the personal accounts of Uriel's presence in people's lives. In times of struggle, sadness, or confusion, Uriel is said to provide healing and comfort to those who call upon him. He is a powerful guardian angel, watching over and protecting his followers from danger. Signs of Uriel's presence have been seen by many, reminding them that they are not alone and that Uriel is always with them. If you ever feel lost or afraid, just remember to call upon Uriel; he will never disappoint you. Believe in Him and His loving guidance; He will lead you toward the light.

Chapter 4: Creating Angelic Sacred Space

Do you feel the presence of angels in your life but don't know how to access their power? Are you seeking a way to honor these spiritual guides and give thanks for their gifts? Creating a sacred space or angelic altar is one way to do this.

By setting up an angelic altar and establishing an intention, you can open the door to angelic blessings, and when you set one up for Uriel, the light of wisdom and protection comes shining through. This chapter will explain how to do it so you can access the energy of Uriel. It will provide practical tools and exercises to help you create an angelic altar that honors the presence of Uriel in your life. The goal is to create a place of peace and protection that allows you to access the divine power and connection with angels. Creating this sacred space and honoring Uriel can open the door to divine blessings.

Creating a Space of Intentional Energy

Angelic altars allow you to connect to a higher power.
https://commons.wikimedia.org/wiki/File:Ottobeuren_basilika_ottobeuren_altar_of_the_guardian_angel_006.JPG

A sacred space or angelic altar is a dedicated area where you can connect with a higher power, meditate, or simply find peace and solace. This space is all about intention and energy, where you create an environment that resonates with the person or entity you want to invite into your life. Whether you're religious, spiritual, or just want a peaceful corner of your home to help you relax and unwind, having a sacred space can benefit you in more ways than you can imagine. This section will explore the significance of creating a sacred space, why intention and energy are crucial, and how to make a space that reflects your personality, where you feel free to be you.

Defining Sacred Space

So, what exactly is a sacred space? Simply put, a sacred space is any designated space that holds significance to an individual or community. This could be a room in your home, a corner of a room, a garden or yard, or any space you feel is significant. The most crucial aspect of any sacred space is the intention behind it. Keeping the energy within that space positive and intentional is crucial, ensuring that every object and detail is there for a reason. Whether creating a space to connect with your higher self or inviting angels and spirits into your life, your intention should be crystal clear before you begin.

Significance of Sacred Space

The significance of creating a sacred space lies in the fact that it provides a physical representation of your connection to the divine. It serves as a reminder of the love and light surrounding you and can also be a powerful tool for manifesting positive change in your life. By having a space dedicated to your spirituality, you are sending a message to the universe that you are ready and willing to receive guidance and support on your life's journey. By spending time in your sacred space, you are creating a place for personal reflection where you stay centered and grounded amid the chaos of daily life.

The Importance of Energy

When creating a space, it is essential to remember the importance of energy. The energy within your space should be a reflection of the intention behind it. Consider the objects that will be within your space. They should all have significance and meaning, such as crystals, candles, and other spiritual tools. Also, take time to consider the colors, textures, and materials you are going to put there. Even the scent of your space can affect the energy within it. Experiment with essential oils or burning incense to create an atmosphere that supports your intention.

Creating a sacred space is all about intention and energy. It is an opportunity to connect with your higher self, the universe, or whichever entity you want to invite into your life. By putting in the time and effort to create a sacred space that is unique and personal to you, you are committing to your spiritual growth and well-being. Remember to keep your intention crystal clear, fill your space with items that have personal meaning, and pay attention to the energy within your space. May your sacred space bring peace, love, and light in all you do.

Setting Up an Angelic Altar

Creating a sacred space for angels is a beautiful way to connect with divine beings and seek their help and guidance. It is a physical representation of our intention and desire to invite angels into our lives. While setting up an altar, choose items that resonate with the energy of the angels to help you feel more connected to them. Let's look at some ways and tools for setting up an angelic sacred space.

Choose a Suitable Location

The first step to creating an angelic altar is to choose a suitable location. Select a place that is peaceful, quiet, and free from distractions. The area should be somewhere you can maintain the altar without it being disturbed by kids or pets. A spare bedroom or corner of your living room might be a good option. The location should be one you can easily access and spend time in to nurture the connection between yourself and the angels.

Selecting Angelic Oracle Cards

Angelic oracle cards are perfect tools for communicating with your angels. They offer insight, inspiration, and guidance from the angels. Choose a set to which you feel drawn and invite the angels to help you select the cards that will help you experience their divine presence. Keep the cards in a box or a special place on your altar so that you can use them when needed. When choosing the cards, ensure that they feel that they are aligned with your intention.

Angel Letters

Angel letters are another powerful tool for connecting with the angels. This is where you write letters to your angels and receive answers by channeling messages from divine beings. Begin by explaining your desires, feelings, or concerns, and write them down. Don't edit them. Just let your feelings run free on the paper. Trust the process and listen for the messages that come from the Angels. You can keep these letters in a notebook or a box on your altar.

Scents and Oils

Scents and oils can be an excellent way to create a conducive environment for angelic communication. You can use incense or essential oils like lavender, frankincense, or myrrh. These scents have calming and soothing properties, which can help you relax and connect with the angels at a deeper level. The scent should be gentle enough not to distract you from your intention and should be soothing and uplifting to your senses.

Crystals

Crystals are beautiful tools for enhancing your connection with the angels. Some of the popular crystals used for this purpose include clear quartz, rose quartz, selenite, and amethyst. These crystals have vibrational energies that can help you feel grounded and connected to the divine. Keep them on your altar, and you can even use them for meditation. In addition, you can hold a crystal in your hand and ask for angelic help and guidance.

Incenses/Sage

Burning fragrant sticks or smudging with sage can purify and purify the air in your space, making it more soothing. Frankincense, lavender, and sandalwood are all great options to try out. Frankincense can enhance your spirituality, while lavender is known for its relaxation properties. When using incense, always open a window or door to allow the smoke to escape. A good practice is to recite an angelic prayer or intention as you light the incense and imagine the rising smoke as the bearer of your wishes.

Angels Statues/Pictures

Since the purpose of this space is to welcome angels, it's a great idea to incorporate angelic decor in your Sacred Space. Angel statues, pictures, or other angelic decor items will invite your desired angelic presence. The visual representation of the celestial beings can comfort and inspire you. Take your time to select the items that capture your connection with your guardian angels. Let your intuition guide you in selecting the items to include.

Healing Music

Music is an essential tool that can help you transform your space. Healing music or calming meditative sounds can create a peaceful and serene environment in your angelic space. Depending on your preference, you can use anything from floral to chakra music. One of the best ways to enjoy this music is by using headphones or earbuds. This way, all the distractions around you will be eliminated, and you will be able to focus entirely on connecting with the angels.

Spiritual Books

Placing spiritual books or oracle cards in your sacred space is also said to promote spiritual growth and well-being. You could read from them before meditating or simply keep them close by. Not only do these items offer guidance for you, but they can also make attractive decor. Place them in a decorative basket or box, and they will look great without taking up too much space. Use them as a reminder to keep your thoughts and intentions aligned with the divine.

Setting up an angelic altar can be a beautiful and transformative experience. It is a sacred space that you can use to connect with the angels, seek guidance, receive messages from the divine, and simply sit in serenely. By selecting suitable items for your altar, you set your intentions and invite the angels to communicate with you. With time and practice, you will learn how to create an environment that fosters a deep and meaningful connection with your angels. Trust your intuition, and let the angels guide you through this beautiful journey.

Exercises for Energetic Protection

As spiritual beings, we often experience moments of vulnerability and emotional turmoil, which let negative entities attach themselves to our aura. When invoking Archangel Uriel, we must prepare ourselves and perform exercises for energetic protection so we are safe from any negativity that may compromise our spiritual journey. This section will explore the different exercises for energetic protection that you can perform to channel the mighty archangel and unleash your inner warrior.

Grounding Exercises

Grounding exercises will also help to keep your energy centered and create a strong foundation for spiritual work. Begin by standing with your feet firmly planted on the ground and visualizing roots extending down to the earth's core. These roots will help you feel connected to the earth and allow negative energies to flow freely from your body. You can also try grounding visualizations that involve standing in the middle of a white light that extends down to the ground.

Shielding Exercises

Shielding exercises help to create a layer of protection around your aura, which keeps any negative entities from attaching themselves to your energy. You can use the power of visualization to create a protective shield around you. Picture a ring of light around your aura that is impenetrable. You can also visualize a white light coming down from Archangel Uriel and surrounding you with his protection.

Breathwork Exercises

Breathing exercises help you reach a deep meditative state, necessary when invoking Archangel Uriel. You do this by taking deep breaths in and out, focusing on the air flowing in and out of your body. Inhale deeply through your nose, hold your breath for a few seconds, and then exhale slowly through your mouth. You can also try alternate nostril breathing exercises that help to balance both hemispheres of your brain.

Mantra and Chanting Exercises

Mantras and chants have been used for centuries to enhance spiritual awareness and protection. You can use a simple chant-like "Om" or "Aum," while meditating to create a vibrational sound that protects your aura. You can also try a mantra used to invoke Archangel Uriel, such as "Uriel, I call upon your protection and guidance," while visualizing yourself surrounded by his light.

Relaxation Exercises

Relaxation exercises help calm the mind and body, which is essential when performing spiritual work. You can use relaxation techniques like yoga, meditation, or tai chi, which help you to become still and focused. This calm state of mind allows you to easily connect with Archangel Uriel and receive his guidance. Along with relaxation exercises, you can also try visualizations that involve picturing yourself surrounded by a peaceful landscape.

Unleashing your inner warrior begins with deepening your spiritual practice and ensuring you are protected against negative entities. These exercises for energetic protection when invoking Uriel will help you achieve a heightened spiritual state, where you can unleash your full potential and connect with Archangel Uriel's wisdom and guidance. Remember to practice each exercise frequently and with intention, just as the greatest warriors always prepare themselves for battle. So, let's prepare ourselves to become spiritual warriors and receive the divine love and protection that Archangel Uriel offers us.

Methods for Enhancing Intention and Achieving Better Focus

As we move towards a society that is constantly on the go, being able to focus, be still, and concentrate on the task at hand has become increasingly difficult. You're not alone if you're struggling to get things done or are constantly being sidetracked. However, it doesn't have to be this way. This section will explore effective methods for enhancing intention and achieving better focus.

Clear Your Mind

The first step towards better focus is to clear your mind of all distractions. Start by creating a to-do list and prioritizing it. This will help you focus on the most crucial tasks first and eliminate unnecessary distractions. Also, clear your physical space of anything that could cause a distraction. As the thoughts come in, don't be afraid to acknowledge them, but then let them go and move on. The more you practice this, the easier it will become.

Practice Mindfulness

Mindfulness is the practice of staying present in the moment, focusing entirely on the task at hand. This means you'll need to eliminate distractions from your surroundings and focus solely on one task. Take deep breaths and stay in the moment, enjoying the feeling of getting things done. If your mind starts to wander, refocus it on what you're doing and take another deep breath. A few minutes of mindfulness each day can make a big difference in your focus and productivity.

Take Breaks

It is vital to take regular breaks throughout the day to re-energize and refresh your mind. This can be as simple as taking a quick walk or stepping outside for a bit of fresh air. Taking breaks will help you maintain your focus throughout the day. When you take a break, make sure to stay away from any potential distractions that can take away your focus. To maximize your break, focus on deep breathing, stretching, or doing something that brings you joy. If you feel overwhelmed, take a few moments to notice and accept your feelings.

Set Goals

Setting specific goals can help you stay motivated and focused. Create daily or weekly goals, and ensure they are specific and measurable. Having something to work towards will keep you focused and motivated. The more achievable your goals are, the more likely you are to stay on track and increase your productivity. A great way to ensure you stay on track is by writing down your goals and tracking your progress.

Eliminate Distractions

Identifying the distractions in your life and eliminating them can be a game-changer in terms of focus. This could mean turning off notifications on your phone, closing unnecessary tabs on your computer, or simply avoiding people or activities that distract you. Bring awareness to all the things that are pulling you away from your task, and make a conscious effort to eliminate them.

Break Up Tasks

Breaking up larger tasks into smaller, more manageable chunks can make tackling them easier. This will help you stay focused on the smaller steps that will eventually lead you to complete the task and feel great about yourself for achieving it. From writing a blog post to getting your taxes done, breaking tasks into smaller chunks can help you stay focused and motivated.

Prioritize Sleep

A good night's rest is vital for optimal focus and productivity. Sleep propels us to stay focused, alert, and motivated. That's why prioritizing good, deep, and refreshing sleep is so important to achieve better focus in your daily life. The chemicals in our brains need time to reset and replenish, so ensure you get enough sleep each night. An early bedtime can make all the difference in your focus and productivity the next day.

Exercise Regularly

Regular exercise can have a huge impact on your focus and productivity. Taking just 30 minutes daily to exercise can increase your mental clarity and overall productivity. The aim is to find something you enjoy and can stick with, which will help you stay motivated. Exercise can also be a great outlet for releasing stress and improving your overall well-being.

Drink Water

Drinking enough water throughout the day can help improve focus and clarity. Dehydration can lead to difficulty focusing, so consuming enough water throughout the day is essential. At least two liters per day is the golden rule for staying hydrated and focusing on the point. A water bottle at your desk will help remind you to drink. Remember that caffeinated drinks should be consumed in moderation and only at certain times of the day.

Practice Gratitude

Practicing gratitude can significantly affect your focus and productivity. Focusing on the positives in life helps you to stay motivated and will intensify your sense of achievement. Write down 3-5 things you are grateful for each day, and consider why you appreciate them. Gratitude can be a powerful way to stay focused and motivated.

While staying focused may be challenging in today's busy world, incorporating these ten methods into your daily routine can greatly enhance your intention and focus. Remember to take breaks, practice mindfulness, and prioritize sleep and exercise. With these simple yet effective tips, you'll be well on your way to better focus and productivity.

There's something truly magical about creating your own angelic sacred space. It's where you can feel at peace, connect with your inner spirituality, and find solace amid a busy world. With a few simple tools and a little imagination, you can transform any space into a serene sanctuary that will renew and refresh you. From crystals and candles to sagging and visualization, there are countless ways to enhance the energy of your space and draw in positive vibes. So go ahead and tap into your creative side; your angelic sacred space is waiting for you!

Chapter 5: Solar Chakra Meditation

The Solar Chakra and Archangel Uriel are two powerful forces that can bring balance and positive energy into your life. The Solar Chakra, also known as the Manipura Chakra, is located in the stomach area and is associated with confidence, self-esteem, and personal power. By focusing on this chakra, you tap into your inner strength, and the result is that you'll feel empowered to pursue your dreams. On the other hand, Archangel Uriel is known as the angel of wisdom and enlightenment. He can help you gain clarity and understanding, and his presence can bring a sense of calm and tranquility to your life.

By combining the power of the solar chakra and Archangel Uriel, you can unleash an amazing amount of potential and achieve greater levels of success and happiness. This chapter focuses on the history and etymology of chakras, how to identify imbalances in the solar plexus chakra and step-by-step meditations for activating and balancing the solar plexus chakra while under the guidance of Archangel Uriel. You will also learn what can be achieved by activating this chakra and how Archangel Uriel can help with the process.

The Mystical World of Chakras

Chakra symbols.
https://pixabay.com/images/id-7182133/

Have you ever wondered about the origins of chakras? What do these energy centers signify, and where do they come from? We are all familiar with the buzzword "chakra," but do we truly understand the depth of their significance? In this section, we will take a historical and etymological dive into the mystical world of chakras, which will give us a comprehensive understanding of these pivotal energy systems.

The word "chakra" finds its origin in the Sanskrit language, which means "wheel" or "disc." The earliest mention of chakras dates back to 1500 BCE when the ancient Hindu text, Vedas, describes chakras as a series of energy points, also known as Padma, meaning lotus flower. These energy points were considered vital for the proper flow of energy within the human body.

Dating back to 600 BCE, according to Buddhist and Hindu traditions, seven primary chakras align with the human spine, stretching from the base to the crown of the head. The seven chakras represent different aspects of human life, including spirituality, creativity, personal power, self-expression, love, communication, and intuition.

The concept of chakras entered the Western world in the 1800s through the Theosophical Society, spreading throughout the world through yoga teachers, mystics, scholars, and spiritual teachers. These ancient energy centers were first mentioned in-depth by the renowned psychoanalyst Carl Jung in his writings, where he valued the importance of accessing the subconscious mind and personal transformation through the chakra.

Several countries view chakras as essential to their cultural and spiritual values. Japanese Reiki, for instance, involves treating and clearing spiritual and physical blockages in the chakras using energy healing modalities. Even Chinese traditional medicine has its system of energy centers, known as meridians.

The significance of chakras has gained immense popularity among Western spiritual seekers in recent times, where they are often associated with vibrational frequency, colors, and sound vibrations. Each chakra possesses its own unique element, frequency, and color to balance the chakra system.

Understanding chakras has evolved over the centuries, and our knowledge of their power continues evolving as we learn more about them. Knowing the historical and etymological background of the chakras helps us understand the importance of energy centers within our body and how they can impact our well-being. As we learn and deepen our understanding of these energy centers, we can better align our body, mind, and spirit to live a fulfilling and balanced life.

The Power of Chakras and Their Angelic Associations

In the world of spirituality and metaphysics, there is no more significant concept than the chakras. They are the wheels of energy that connect our physical body and our consciousness. They are said to be the centers of our emotional and spiritual well-being and help balance our energy flows, which affect our emotional health. This section will discuss each chakra's attributes and physical connections, including their angelic associations. Are you ready to unlock the power of your chakras and achieve spiritual balance? Keep reading to find out more.

1. The root chakra, or Muladhara, is the first chakra located at the spine's base. The color associated with this chakra is red, and its attributes are grounding, stability, and security. Archangel Michael is the angelic association of the root chakra, known for his protective qualities. Physical activities such as yoga, walking, or gardening are recommended to balance this chakra.

2. The sacral chakra, or Swadhisthana, is located below the navel and is associated with orange. This chakra is responsible for our sexual energy, creativity, and passion. Archangel Gabriel is the angelic association of the sacral chakra. He is known for his wealth of creativity and inspiration. Balance this chakra with activities such as dancing, painting, or any other creative outlet that resonates with you.

3. The solar plexus chakra, or *Manipura,* is located behind the navel and is associated with yellow. This chakra is responsible for our personal power, confidence, and self-esteem. Archangel Uriel is the angelic association of the solar plexus chakra, known for bringing clarity and purpose into our lives. Try practicing self-care activities such as journaling, meditation, or affirmations to balance this chakra.
4. The heart chakra, Anahata, is located at the center of the chest and is associated with the color green. This chakra is responsible for our love, compassion, and forgiveness. Archangel Chamuel is the angelic association of the Heart chakra, known for its healing properties. To balance this chakra, spend time in nature, practice gratitude, and show kindness to yourself and others.
5. The throat chakra, Vishuddha, is located at the base of the neck and is associated with the color blue. This chakra is responsible for communication, self-expression, and authenticity. Archangel Gabriel is the angelic association of the throat chakra, known for his ability to bring clarity and truth. To balance this chakra, practice singing, public speaking, or any other form of self-expression that speaks to your soul.

The power of chakras and their angelic associations can be life-changing. By acknowledging and understanding each chakra's attributes and physical connections, we can tap into our spiritual energy and unlock our full potential. Take some time to explore each chakra and try different activities that resonate with you. You never know; you just might find the key to unlocking your inner peace and finding your purpose!

Archangel Uriel and the Solar Plexus Chakra

Have you ever wondered about the connection between the Archangels and our chakras? Our chakras are the energy centers in our bodies related to our physical, emotional, and spiritual well-being. Archangels are celestial beings who guide us toward a life full of positivity and love. In this section, we will explore the connection between Archangel Uriel and the solar plexus chakra, the third chakra located in the upper abdomen.

Archangel Uriel is known as the angel of wisdom and enlightenment and is often depicted in association with the sun's power. He embodies the qualities of confidence, courage, and self-esteem. The solar plexus chakra represents our personal power, confidence, and self-worth. When these two entities come together, they create a powerful force that can help us achieve our goals and lead a life full of self-confidence.

The solar plexus chakra is associated with the element of fire, which signifies transformation and change. When we open up this chakra, we let go of old patterns and beliefs and welcome new ideas and possibilities that lead us to our greatest purpose. Archangel Uriel can help us in this process of change and transformation by guiding us toward our inner wisdom and illuminating our path.

If you feel your self-worth has been shaken and your confidence has taken a hit, it could indicate a blocked solar plexus chakra. Archangel Uriel can help you unblock the chakra and give you the strength to move forward. By invoking his presence and repeating affirmations like, "I am confident in my power," we can connect with the angel's energy and heal ourselves.

Moreover, Archangel Uriel can also help us overcome the anxiety and stress often associated with an imbalanced solar plexus chakra. By visualizing a golden light surrounding us and focusing on our breathing, we can invite Archangel Uriel to fill us with his light, which helps to balance our chakra and calm our nerves.

The connection between Archangel Uriel and the solar plexus chakra can help us strengthen our sense of self-worth and lead a life full of purpose and positivity. By including simple practices in our daily routine, we can connect with Archangel Uriel's sound spirit and allow ourselves to receive his divine guidance. Take a moment to connect with your solar plexus chakra, feel the presence of Archangel Uriel, and let him guide you toward your greatest potential.

Identifying Unbalances in the Solar Plexus Chakra

Have you ever felt as if you are stuck in a rut, unable to move forward in life? Do you often struggle with decision-making, lack self-confidence, or experience digestive issues? These may be signs that your Solar Plexus Chakra, which governs personal power and self-esteem, is unbalanced.

This section will discuss identifying the imbalance in this chakra and exploring ways to restore harmony.

- When balanced, the solar plexus chakra helps us feel confident in our abilities, make decisions with ease, and have a sense of purpose. However, when it is unbalanced, it can result in a lack of direction, energy, and self-esteem, amongst other things
- One of the most common signs of an unbalanced solar plexus chakra is a digestive issue related to the stomach and pancreas. This can show up as constipation, diarrhea, acid reflux or indigestion, and a lack of appetite. Additionally, you may experience physical symptoms such as ulcers, infections, and liver or kidney problems
- Another sign of an unbalanced solar plexus chakra is a lack of self-confidence. You may find yourself doubting your abilities or feeling like an imposter. This lack of confidence can prevent you from taking risks, achieving your goals, and pursuing your dreams. You may also find yourself seeking validation from others instead of trusting your judgment
- Decision-making can also be difficult when this chakra is unbalanced. You may find yourself struggling to make even small decisions, like what to eat for dinner or which movie to watch. This indecisiveness can lead to analysis paralysis and prevent you from taking action toward your goals
- Increased stress and anxiety levels can also indicate an unbalanced solar plexus chakra. When this chakra is overactive, it can lead to a constant feeling of stress or anxiety, which can manifest as physical symptoms such as headaches and muscle tension

Identifying imbalances in the solar plexus chakra can help you understand why you may be experiencing certain physical or emotional symptoms. Once you recognize these imbalances, you can take steps to restore balance. Some ways to do this include practicing yoga or meditation, eating a balanced diet, engaging in physical activity, and setting boundaries for yourself. Remember that restoring balance takes time and patience, so be kind to yourself as you start this journey. Dedication and practice can bring harmony and peace back to your solar plexus chakra, helping you live your best life.

Step-by-Step Meditations for Activating and Balancing the Solar Plexus Chakra

Do you often feel overwhelmed, anxious, or insecure? These are common symptoms of a blocked solar plexus chakra, the energy center located in the upper abdomen. This chakra can help you feel confident, empowered, and at peace with yourself when activated and balanced. You can heal this chakra and, again, overall well-being through meditation. In this section, we'll guide you through step-by-step meditations to help you activate and balance your solar plexus chakra for inner peace.

Breathing Meditation

Meditation can start with a simple technique called breathing meditation. It helps you become more aware of your breath and control your thoughts. Sit in a comfortable place, close your eyes, and breathe deeply. Mentally observe your breath and focus your mind on the sensations. Let any thoughts that arise fade away peacefully. Take this time to be mindful and connect with your breath.

Solar Plexus Visualization Meditation

Visualize a bright yellow sun resting within your solar plexus chakra. Close your eyes and focus your attention on the area. Imagine a bright beam of sunlight that flows from the sun in your chakra and spreads throughout your body. Allow the light to transform any negative emotions into positive ones, such as self-confidence, courage, and empowerment. Staying focused on this visualization for a few minutes or until you feel your solar plexus chakra energized is vital.

Chanting Meditation

This chakra is also associated with the sound of "Ram." Chant this sound repeatedly while breathing deeply. As you chant, imagine the vibration moving through your solar plexus and spreading throughout your body. Let the sound fill you with confidence and inner strength. As you chant, your solar plexus chakra will become more balanced.

Affirmation Meditation

Repeat positive affirmations that align with the qualities of the solar plexus chakra. Say things like "I am confident, I am worthy, I am powerful." Feel the energy of the affirmations spreading through your body, filling you with positive energy. Say each phrase confidently and confidently until you feel your solar plexus chakra activated.

Yoga Meditation

Yoga is a great way to balance all the body's chakras, including the solar plexus chakra. Incorporate yoga postures like the Boat Pose, Warrior 1, and Surya Namaskar, which focus on strengthening your core, creating space in the solar plexus region, and activating the energy flow to the chakra.

Meditation is a holistic way to balance, heal, and activate the body's chakras. When you focus on the solar plexus chakra, you can find peace and confidence within yourself. Use these step-by-step meditations to activate and balance your solar plexus chakra to promote overall well-being. As you continue to practice these meditations regularly, you will notice positive changes in your body, mind, and soul. Rejoice in this journey of healing and finding inner peace!

Harness the Power of Your Solar Plexus Chakra

The human body is a complex system of energy centers known as chakras that play a vital role in our physical, emotional, and spiritual well-being. The solar plexus chakra or Manipura Chakra is considered the center of your personal power and self-esteem. This chakra governs your willpower, confidence, and decision-making abilities. It is said that when the solar plexus chakra is balanced, you will feel confident, centered, and self-assured. This section will explore the benefits of activating your solar plexus chakra and how it can lead to success and abundance.

- **Increased Confidence and Willpower:** When your solar plexus chakra is balanced, you will feel a sense of confidence and personal power. You will have the willpower to achieve your goals and the confidence to follow through on them. This will help you make better decisions and live a more fulfilling life
- **Improved Digestion and Metabolism**: The solar plexus chakra is associated with the digestive system, and when it is balanced, it can improve your digestion and metabolism. You will have better assimilation of nutrients and a healthier gut, leading to an overall improvement in your health

- **Personal And Professional Success:** Activating your solar plexus chakra can lead to personal and professional success. You will be able to take charge of your life, make clearer decisions, and act toward reaching your goals. This will lead to a sense of accomplishment, higher productivity, and an overall sense of success
- **Release of Anger and Emotional Healing:** When the solar plexus chakra is balanced, it helps release negative emotions such as anger, resentment, and frustration. This clears the path for emotional healing and can profoundly impact your life. You will feel more peaceful, happy, and balanced
- **Improved Self-Esteem**: One of the main benefits of activating your solar plexus chakra is improved self-esteem. When your chakra is balanced, you will have a strong connection with your inner self, leading to better self-awareness, self-acceptance, and higher self-esteem

The solar plexus chakra is a powerful energy center that can profoundly impact your physical, emotional, and spiritual well-being. By activating this chakra, you can tap into your power and achieve success and abundance in all areas of your life. Developing a daily practice that includes meditation, affirmations, and yoga can help balance your solar plexus chakra and improve confidence, self-esteem, and personal growth. So go ahead and harness the power of your solar plexus chakra today!

How Can Archangel Uriel Help with Activating the Solar Chakra

Archangel Uriel is the perfect helper for activating your Solar Chakra! As one of the seven archangels, Uriel is known for his incredible ability to ignite a sense of peace and enlightenment in those who seek his assistance. Regarding your Solar Chakra, Uriel's powerful energy can help you tap into your inner wisdom and confidence. With his guidance, you can tap into the sun's power that resides within you, unleashing your full potential and inner radiance. Let Archangel Uriel be your guiding light, and watch your Solar Chakra shine brighter than ever!

Along with connecting with Archangel Uriel, there are other things you can do to activate your solar chakra. Eating yellow foods like bananas, pineapples, and squash can help stimulate this chakra. Practicing yoga poses such as the warrior or the sun salutation can also help. In addition, spending time in nature, especially in the sunshine, can boost this energy center.

Connecting with Archangel Uriel can be a powerful way to activate the solar chakra and achieve greater harmony and balance. As you work with the energies of Archangel Uriel and focus on solar chakra activation, you may discover that you have increased energy, motivation, and creativity. Activating this chakra takes time and effort, *so be patient with yourself and continue your practice.* With Archangel Uriel's guidance, you can unlock your true potential and live a more fulfilling life.

Chapter 6: Fire-in-Palm Meditation

If you're a fan of meditation, chances are you've tried various techniques to help you relax and clear your mind. But have you ever heard of the fire-in-palm meditation? This unique practice can help you release stress and negative emotions, leaving you feeling lighter and more focused. Taking just a few minutes out of your day to complete a session of fire-in-palm meditation can make all the difference to your emotional and spiritual well-being. By focusing on your breath and being present in the moment, you can tap into the spiritual realm and draw on a vast well of positive energy for healing and peace of mind.

This section will provide a step-by-step guide to achieving the fire-in-palm meditation. By connecting with Archangel Uriel, you can release any negative energy and achieve emotional healing. This chapter will explore how to find a quiet place for meditation, set an intention, clear your mind, and practice fire-in-palm meditation. Also, ways to take your practice further and ways that will encourage you to reflect on the experience will be looked at. By the time you're done reading, you will have a firm understanding of the fire-in-palm method and how it can be used to achieve emotional healing.

Preparing for Fire-in-Palm Meditation

Meditation can reduce stress.
https://unsplash.com/photos/vs-PjCh5goo?utm_source=unsplash&utm_medium=referral&utm_content=creditShareLink

Many forms of meditation bring relaxation, focus, and inner peace to your life. Fire in palm meditation is an ancient practice that has been used for centuries to clear the mind, reduce stress, and improve overall well-being. To effectively practice fire-in-palm meditation, there are a few steps to take before you start.

Setting Your Intention

Once you have found your quiet place, take some time to connect with your intention for the fire-in-palm meditation. This could be a phrase, word, or feeling you want to focus on during your meditation. It is helpful to write it down on a piece of paper and keep it close by so you can refer to it if you need to during your meditation. Setting an intention will help you to stay focused throughout the practice.

Clearing Your Mind

When preparing for fire-in-palm meditation, clearing your mind of distractions and clutter is essential. You can start by taking a few deep breaths and focusing on your breath. Try to release any thoughts or feelings that may interfere with your practice. Visualize yourself releasing any negative energies or emotions by allowing yourself to be surrounded by love, light, and positivity.

Body Preparation

In fire-in-palm meditation practice, you focus on the palms of your hand. Gently touch your fingertips to your palms, and visualize a flame burning brightly in the center of your palm. The flame serves as a focal point during the meditation, and as you inhale, imagine that you're bringing the flame's energy into your body, and as you exhale, allow it to surround and protect you. You could also do physical exercises like stretching or yoga to prepare your body for meditation before practicing fire in the palm.

Commitment to Consistency

As with any meditation practice, consistency is key in the fire-in-palm practice. This means committing to practice regularly, whether daily, once a week, or twice a month. The frequency of your practice is up to you, but the important thing is to stay committed and consistent. You'll find that the more you practice, the easier it becomes, and the greater the benefits.

Fire-in-palm meditation is a dynamic practice that can help you find peace, reduce stress, and improve your overall well-being. This section has shared some useful tips for preparing yourself for this meditation practice. Remember, finding a quiet place, setting your intention, clearing your mind, and committing to consistency are key. With regular practice, fire-in-palm meditation can help you connect with your inner self and Archangel Uriel and find a sense of calm in your everyday life.

Practicing Fire-in-Palm Meditation

When it comes to palm meditation, it is all about practicing the power of visualization. It is a unique form of meditation to help you focus your mind, increase your intuition, and connect with your inner self. This section will give you a step-by-step guide on how to practice fire-in-palm meditation.

Step 1: Find a Peaceful Place

The first step towards preparing for fire-in-palm is to find a quiet place where you can be alone and undisturbed. This could be a room in your house, an outdoor space, or a designated meditation room. The important thing is to find a peaceful and quiet space where you can be free from distractions. Ensure you're sitting comfortably and the environment is conducive to meditation.

Step 2: Take a Deep Breath

Now that you have found a peaceful place, sit comfortably and take deep breaths. Close your eyes and relax your body. Take long, deep breaths in and out, allowing your body and mind to calm down. Notice how your breathing slows as you become more relaxed. Notice the rise and fall of your chest as you inhale and exhale. Take a few more deep breaths before continuing with your practice.

Step 3: Visualizing the Fire in Your Palms

Once you have relaxed your body and mind, visualize the fire in your palms. Imagine flames burning brightly in the center of both palms and letting the heat spread throughout your body. Visualize the warmth and glow emanating from your palms, and breathe in deeply, feeling the warmth spread throughout your body. Take a few more deep breaths and allow the heat to envelop your entire body. Feel the warmth as it calms your mind and relaxes your muscles.

Step 4: Connecting with Archangel Uriel

Next, you will want to connect with Archangel Uriel. He is associated with the element of fire and can help you connect with your inner self. Say a prayer to Archangel Uriel and ask him to guide you in your meditation. You can light a candle or incense and place it before you to help you connect more closely with the Archangel. The prayer can be as simple or as detailed as you wish.

Step 5: Repeat and Reflect

Continue to visualize the fire in your palms and connect with Archangel Uriel for as long as you like. Take your time and enjoy the process. When you have finished, take a few minutes to reflect on your practice. How did it make you feel? Did any insights or newfound clarity come to you during the meditation? Write your thoughts or feelings in a journal to help you reflect on future meditations.

Finally, take some deep breaths and open your eyes slowly. You should feel more relaxed and at peace. Fire in palm meditation is a potent practice that can help you find inner peace, reduce stress, and improve your overall well-being. With regular practice, you'll soon be able to experience the healing and peace of mind that comes with connecting with Archangel Uriel. Remember to take your time and allow yourself to fully immerse yourself in the experience. You'll develop greater intuition, clarity, and focus on your daily life. So, take a deep breath, light the fire in your palms, and connect with Archangel Uriel.

After the Fire-in-Palm Meditation

Once you have finished your fire-in-palm meditation, take some time to center yourself and get grounded. You may want to drink water or walk outside to help you come back into, and reconnect with, your body. There are a few other things to remember when you come out of your meditation. In this section, we will explore how practicing fire-in-palm meditation can transform your life in three ways.

Reflection and Gratitude

The fire-in-palm meditation is about visualizing a flame, reflecting on your emotions, and practicing gratitude. When you visualize the flame, you also visualize all the things that no longer serve you, such as stress, worry, and negative thoughts. You are then encouraged to release these negative energies and bring positivity by focusing on things you are grateful for. This practice helps you develop a positive mindset and connect with your inner self, which can lead to a happier and more fulfilling life.

Releasing Your Intentions

Another powerful aspect of the fire-in-palm meditation is the ability to release your intentions and offer them to Archangel Uriel. While visualizing the flame, you can focus on what you wish for, whether it's for personal growth, relationships, or career aspirations. By releasing your intentions to the universe, you are creating a positive energy that attracts what you desire. This allows you to manifest your desires and achieve your goals.

Feeling Empowered

The fire-in-palm meditation can also leave you feeling empowered. As you visualize the flame, you are also visualizing the power that comes with it, which will reverberate within you. This practice helps you tap into your inner strength and, together with the help of Uriel, gives you the courage to face challenges and overcome obstacles. Feeling empowered makes you more likely to take action toward what you want in life and achieve success.

In summary, fire-in-palm meditation is a powerful tool that can transform your life in several ways. By practicing this meditation, you can reflect on your emotions and practice gratitude, release your intentions, and feel empowered. These benefits can lead to a happier and more fulfilling life. So, next time you sit down to meditate, try the fire-in-palm meditation and see the positive changes it can bring to your life.

The Art of Grounding

In our busy, fast-paced lives, becoming disconnected from what truly matters is easy. We spend so much time with our heads buried in screens or rushing from one activity to the next that we forget to slow down and connect with the world around us. That's where grounding comes in. Taking the time to be still, breathe, and connect with nature can help us realign with our true selves, gain perspective, and cultivate peace of mind. Grounding is a practice that dates back centuries, but it's just as relevant in today's world as it ever was. Let's explore what grounding is, why it's important, and how you can cultivate your practice of grounding.

What Is Grounding?

Grounding is a natural way of reconnecting with the earth and the present moment. It involves intentionally and mindfully connecting with the physical world around us, whether that's through walking barefoot on grass, taking a walk in the forest, or simply sitting outside and breathing in the fresh air. This practice can help us feel more centered, more rooted, and more connected to our environment.

Why Is Grounding Important?

Grounding can benefit us in many ways, both physically and mentally. Studies have shown that practicing grounding can reduce stress, improve sleep quality, and boost immune function. It can also help us feel more grateful, joyful, and present daily. Plus, it's a simple and accessible practice that anyone can do with no special equipment or training required.

When invoking Archangel Uriel during the fire-in-palm meditation, grounding is important because it helps create a safe and sacred space for you. A grounded presence will ensure you are open and receptive to Archangel Uriel's healing energies. The more grounded you can be, the easier for him to send you his love and healing light.

Cultivating Your Practice of Grounding

The key to grounding is creating an intentional and mindful connection with the physical world around you. The good news is that there are many ways to ground yourself, and you can experiment to find what works best for you. Some popular grounding practices include:

- Walking barefoot on grass, sand, or soil
- Hugging a tree and feeling its energy
- Listening to the sounds of nature – birds, water, wind, etc.
- Sitting or lying on the ground and feeling its support
- Practicing mindfulness meditation and focusing on your breath

Whichever practice you choose, try to make it a regular habit or ritual. Set aside time each day or each week to connect with nature and yourself. Remember, grounding is a practice, and it may take time and effort to find what works for you, but the rewards are well worth it.

Benefits of a Regular Grounding Practice

While grounding can be beneficial in the short term, it has even greater potential when practiced regularly over time. Regularly connecting with nature can bring a sense of well-being and peace into our lives, which can have a ripple effect on all aspects of life. As we ground ourselves more often, we become more aware of our surroundings and more in tune with ourselves. We can experience increased energy, improved mood, and greater clarity of thought. Plus, grounding can help us to better manage our stress levels and cultivate loving relationships with ourselves and others.

- **Reduced Stress and Anxiety**: By connecting with nature regularly, we can become better attuned to ourselves and our environment. This helps us to manage stress in healthy ways and reduce feelings of anxiousness
- **Improved Sleep Quality:** Regular breaks to ground ourselves can help us feel more relaxed before bedtime, resulting in better quality sleep.
- **Boosted Immune Function:** Studies have shown that grounding can help to boost our immune system and reduce inflammation in the body.

- **Increased Mindfulness and Presence:** Regular grounding makes us more mindful of our thoughts and feelings. This makes it easier to be present in the moment and appreciate the beauty of our surroundings.
- **Enhanced Feelings of Gratitude and Joy:** Grounding can help us recognize and appreciate the small things, which can bring more joy into our lives.
- **Connection with Nature and Community:** As we ground ourselves more often, we open up to the beauty and energy of nature around us. This can lead to stronger connections with ourselves, our environment, and the people in our lives.

Regularly grounding yourself creates a greater sense of peace, stillness, and connection in your life. You'll feel more centered no matter what challenges come your way. Plus, you'll appreciate the beauty and wonder of the world around you.

Grounding is a powerful practice that reconnects us with ourselves, our environment, and the present moment. Whether you're feeling stressed, anxious, or simply seeking a greater sense of peace and stillness, grounding can be a valuable tool. Take time each day to connect with nature, breathe deeply, and feel your feet on the ground. You might be surprised at how much of a difference it can make in your overall well-being.

Taking the Fire in Palm Meditation Further

Fire in palm meditation has its roots in Buddhism and Taoism. It is a simple yet potent practice accessible to anyone who wants to connect with their inner self and awaken their spiritual consciousness. This meditation is especially beneficial for people who are going through a stressful time in their lives and want to find inner peace and clarity. If you've been practicing the fire-in-palm meditation for a while and want to take your practice to the next level, creating a powerful mantra is one way to do so. This section will explore how to create a mantra and how to take your fire-in-palm meditation practice further by practicing with others and growing your spiritual practice.

Creating a Mantra

A mantra is a word or phrase repeated during meditation to focus your mind and help you reach a state of inner peace and relaxation, connect with your subconscious, and unlock your spiritual potential. To create your mantra, start by reflecting on your intentions and goals for your meditation practice. What do you want to achieve? What qualities do you want to cultivate in yourself? Once you clearly sense your intentions, choose a word or phrase that embodies these qualities. Some examples of powerful mantras include "I am peace," "I am love," "I am strength," "I am grateful," and "I am limitless." Repeat your mantra during meditation and notice how it affects your state of mind and overall experience.

Practicing with Others

While the fire-in-palm meditation is typically practiced alone, there are benefits to practicing with others. When you practice with others, you can create a supportive community of like-minded individuals who share your goals and aspirations. You can also learn from each other and deepen your spiritual practice together. To find a community of fire-in-palm meditation practitioners, look for local meditation groups in your area or join online communities. You can also organize your group by inviting friends, family, or colleagues to meditate with you. Set a regular schedule for your group meditation sessions and experiment with different meditation techniques, such as guided meditations, mantra meditations, and visualization meditations.

Growing Your Spiritual Practice

Fire in palm meditation is just one of many spiritual practices that can help you connect with your inner self and awaken your spiritual potential. To take your spiritual practice further, consider exploring other practices such as yoga, mindfulness, tai chi, or qigong. These practices can complement your meditation practice and help you cultivate a deeper sense of balance, harmony, and well-being. You can also explore different aspects of your spirituality, such as exploring different religions, learning about energy healing, or connecting with nature. Remember, spirituality is a personal journey that's unique to each individual. Listen to your intuition, follow your heart as you explore new paths, and deepen your connection with your inner self.

Fire in palm meditation is a powerful practice that can help you connect with your inner self and awaken your spiritual consciousness. By creating a powerful mantra, practicing with others, and exploring other spiritual practices, you can take your fire-in-palm meditation practice to the next level and deepen your overall spiritual practice. Remember, there is no one-size-fits-all approach when it comes to spirituality. Listen to your intuition and follow your heart as you discover new ways to connect with your inner self and the world around you.

Chapter 7: Dreamwork

Are you ready to tap into the guidance of Archangel Uriel through your dreams? Dreamwork is a powerful tool for communicating with angels, and with some intention and practice, you can learn to connect with Archangel Uriel while you sleep. Whether you're looking for insight on a particular issue or seeking to deepen your spiritual awakening, Archangel Uriel can help. Nighttime can be a powerful ground for guidance and growth, so allow yourself to relax and let the wisdom of Archangel Uriel guide you.

Dreams can help you connect with Uriel.
https://unsplash.com/photos/rUc9hVE-L-E?utm_source=unsplash&utm_medium=referral&utm_content=creditShareLink

This chapter will introduce you to the concept of dreamwork, provide step-by-step exercises to connect with Archangel Uriel in your dreams and suggest some tips for creating the best environment possible to make the most of your dreamwork. The purpose is to help you gain access to Archangel Uriel's loving and healing energy, making your dreamtime a powerful ally in creating the life of your dreams. By the end of this chapter, you'll be equipped with practical tools and techniques to make the most of your dreamtime.

Defining Dreamwork

Have you ever woken up from a dream feeling like it was trying to tell you something? Dreams have fascinated humans for centuries, and dreamwork has been used as a tool for self-exploration, healing, and problem-solving for years. But what is dreamwork, and how can it help us? To help you understand the power of dreamwork, this section will define it, explore its benefits, and lay out some techniques to start working with your dreams.

What Is Dreamwork?

Dreamwork is the process of analyzing and interpreting dreams to gain a deeper understanding of the self and one's emotions. Through dreamwork, we can unlock our dreams' hidden meanings and symbols to help us navigate life's challenges. Whether you believe that dreams are a window into our subconscious or simply a reflection of our daily experiences, there is no denying the power of dreamwork in helping us to live our best lives. It is essentially the practice of analyzing and understanding the messages within our dreams. These messages can give us insight into our subconscious mind, emotions, desires, and even physical health. It can be done alone, but it's often more effective with the guidance of a therapist or a trained dream facilitator.

Benefits of Dreamwork

So why is dreamwork so beneficial? For starters, dreams can reflect what we're going through in our waking life. By analyzing the patterns and themes in our dreams, we can better understand our inner selves and the challenges we face. Dreams can also offer solutions to problems that we may not have been able to access otherwise. Here are some benefits of dreamwork:

- Gain insight into your subconscious mind and emotions
- Understand recurring themes in your dreams
- Receive creative solutions to problems
- Connect with the spiritual realm
- Heal and overcome trauma

Dreamwork may initially seem intimidating and complicated, but it can be a powerful tool for self-discovery and healing. There isn't a right or wrong way to approach dreamwork, it's based on your dreams, so it's a personal journey that you can tailor to your own needs and preferences. Whether you choose to work with a therapist or explore dreamwork on your own, listening to your dreams can bring a new level of self-knowledge and awareness to your life. So, the next time you wake up from a dream feeling like it's trying to tell you something, don't ignore it. Take the time to explore its meaning and see where it might lead you.

Dreamwork Techniques

Some people believe that their dreams can give insights into their subconscious thoughts and emotions, while others see dreams as a source of creative inspiration. Dreamwork techniques help people explore and understand their dreams, harnessing the power of their subconscious mind. This section will explore some of the most popular dreamwork techniques and how they can help you unlock your inner dreamer.

Dream Journaling

Keeping a dream journal is one of the most effective ways to improve your dream recall and analysis. Writing down your dreams immediately after waking up helps you retain more details and remember your dreams vividly. You can also use your dream journal to reflect on recurring themes or symbols in your dreams, giving you a clear idea of what is going on in your subconscious.

Lucid Dreaming

Lucid dreaming is a state where you become aware that you are dreaming, allowing you to control and manipulate the dream. With practice, you can learn how to induce lucid dreams and use them to explore your inner world. Lucid dreaming can also help you overcome fears or anxieties by facing them in a controlled environment.

Dream Imagery

Dream imagery is a technique that involves visualizing dream symbols and re-imagining them to get more knowledge of yourself. By revisiting a dream and altering certain elements, you can uncover hidden thoughts and emotions that your subconscious mind is trying to communicate. Dream imagery is particularly helpful for working through emotional issues or trauma.

Active Imagination

An active imagination is a method that uses guided meditation or visualization to explore your unconscious. In this practice, you allow your mind to wander freely and follow the images and thoughts that arise. Active imagination encourages you to embrace spontaneity and let go of analytical thinking, promoting a more intuitive and creative approach to exploring your dreams.

Group Dreamwork

Group dreamwork involves sharing your dreams with others and exchanging information and interpretations. By hearing different perspectives on your dreams, you can better understand their meaning and connect with others who share your interests. Group dreamwork can also offer a safe and supportive environment for processing complex emotions or experiences.

Dreamwork techniques are valuable tools for anyone interested in exploring their subconscious and tapping into their inner creativity. By keeping a dream journal, practicing lucid dreaming, using dream imagery or active imagination, and participating in group dreamwork, you can gain new insights into your psyche and understand yourself more deeply.

How Dreams Connect to Angelic Communication

Have you ever had dreams that seem so real that you can't shake the thought of them off when you wake up? Dreams that leave you feeling like there's something more to them than just a mere reflection of your thoughts? Dreams that connect you to a higher power? These dreams could be a way for you to communicate with angels. This section will explore the connection between your dreams and angelic communication and how you can decipher their messages.

Angels often communicate with us through dreams because it's the most natural way to do it. They're pure beings made of light and energy, and they can't communicate with us through the physical realm. Dreams, on the other hand, provide a gateway into the spiritual realm, where angels reside. Our minds are open to receiving messages from the divine when we're asleep, making it an ideal opportunity for angels to communicate with us.

When you have a dream involving angels, pay attention to the dream's details. Notice the messages and symbols that appear. These messages could be literal messages from an angel or hold a hidden meaning that only you can decipher. Angels often use symbols like feathers, rainbows, and numbers to communicate with us, so pay attention to these details in your dreams.

Your intuition is a powerful tool for decoding your dreams. Angels frequently use your intuition to communicate with you. Feeling a sense of peace and comfort during a dream could signify that an angel is reaching out to you. Similarly, if you have a dream that encourages you to explore new opportunities, it could be a way for angels to guide you toward a new direction in life.

One of the key things that angels want to communicate with us is that we're never alone. They're always with us, offering guidance and support whenever we need it. Dreams can be a way to remind us of this fact. If you're feeling overwhelmed with life's challenges, ask the angelic realm for guidance and pay attention to your dreams. You might receive a message that brings you peace and reassurance.

When decoding your dreams, there's no right or wrong way to do it. Everyone's experiences are unique, and it's up to you to find the meaning that resonates with you. However, remember that angels are always here to guide and support us. By paying attention to our dreams and connecting with the angelic realm, we can receive the guidance we need to reach our full potential.

Dreams are a very powerful way to communicate with the angelic realm. Angels often use them because it's a natural way to connect with us on a spiritual level. By paying attention to the messages and symbols in our dreams, we can decipher the hidden messages from angels. Our intuition is a valuable tool for decoding our dreams, and it is important to trust our instincts when understanding the messages. Remember that angels are always here to guide and support us, and our dreams can be a way to receive their messages.

Steps to Connecting with Archangel Uriel Through Dreams

There are many ways to connect with the spiritual world, and Archangel Uriel is one of the most sought-after angels. One of the most powerful ways to connect with him is through your dreams. The dream world, the gateway to our subconscious, can be used to communicate with the spiritual world, and this section will explore the steps you can take to connect with Archangel Uriel.

1. **Set an Intention:** The first step in connecting with Archangel Uriel through dreamwork is to set your intention. Before going to bed, take a few moments to set your intention by simply saying a prayer or setting an intention in your mind. This will help you to be more receptive to his presence in your dreams.

2. **Use Affirmations:** Affirmations are a powerful way to set your subconscious mind into action. Before you go to bed, repeat affirmations such as, "I am open to connecting with Archangel Uriel in my dreams tonight" or "I am ready to receive guidance from Archangel Uriel in my dreams." This will help you align your mind with your intentions. The more frequently you use affirmations, the more likely you will receive guidance from Uriel in your dreams.

3. **Practice Visualization:** Visualization is a powerful tool to help you connect with Archangel Uriel. Before you go to bed, close your eyes, and visualize Archangel Uriel standing before you. Feel his presence and invite him to communicate with you in your dreams. This will set the stage for a powerful dream experience. When you start to drift off to sleep, focus on the visualization you have created and allow yourself to relax in his presence.

4. **Keep a Dream Journal:** As soon as you wake up, write down any dreams you remember. This will help you remember your dreams more vividly and allow you to analyze them later. When you write down your dreams, include any

symbols that stood out to you, as they may be a message from Archangel Uriel. Try to write down as much detail about the dream as possible. If you feel something important is missing, take a few moments to meditate and allow yourself to become fully present in the dream.

5. **Interpret Your Dreams:** After writing down your dreams, take some time to interpret their meaning. Ask yourself what the symbols mean, how they make you feel, and if there is a message in the dream that Archangel Uriel may be trying to communicate with you. Interpretations can vary from person to person, so it is crucial to find the meaning that resonates most with you. Some people also like to consult dream dictionaries for additional guidance.

6. **Be Patient and Persistent:** Connecting with Archangel Uriel through your dreams may take time and practice. Remember that not every dream will have a message from him, but that doesn't mean he isn't trying to communicate with you. Be patient and persistent in your efforts to connect with him, and trust that the messages will come to you when the time is right. The more you trust in yourself and the process, the easier it will be to receive Archangel Uriel's guidance.

Connecting with Archangel Uriel through your dreams is a powerful way to receive messages and guidance. By firmly setting your intention, keeping a dream journal, practicing visualization, using affirmations, and being patient and persistent, you can open the door to meaningful communication with Archangel Uriel. Remember, connecting with the spiritual world takes time and practice, so keep at it, and you'll be amazed at the messages and inspiration that come through your dreams.

Using a Dream Journal

Dreams can reveal our deepest fears, desires, and thoughts that we might not even be aware of. Archangel Uriel often uses dreams to communicate messages, so keeping track of your dreams in a dream journal is important. That's why keeping a journal can be an amazing tool for self-discovery, personal growth, and connection with Archangel Uriel. This section will explain the benefits of keeping a dream journal and give you tips on how to start one.

Set a Schedule

The first step to starting a dream journal is to set a schedule. Decide how often you want to write in your journal and how much time you want to dedicate to writing each entry. Choose a time and day that works best for you and stick to it. This will help create the habit of recording your dreams. Once you get into the habit, it will become easier. When you start your dream journal, make sure to include some basic information, like the date and time of the dream, how you felt before you went to bed, and any other information that might be important.

Write Down Your Dreams

Start by recording what stood out most in your dreams: characters, emotions, places, colors, and anything else that stands out to you. Don't forget to include the symbols and messages that Archangel Uriel might be sending you. These can be subtle but very powerful. It's also important to include any feelings or emotions you experienced during the dream. These can give you further insight into the messages that Archangel Uriel is sending you.

Understanding Your Dreams

Dreams can be confusing and fragmented, making it difficult to decipher their meaning. However, by writing your dreams down in a journal, you can identify any emerging patterns and themes. You'll also be able to reflect on particular events or feelings that may have triggered certain dreams. If you have trouble understanding the message of your dream, try writing it down in a story format to help make sense of it. This will also make it easier to identify symbols and themes that appear throughout your dreams.

Record Your Reflections

Once you've written down the details of your dream, take a few moments to think about it. This is a great time to let your intuition free and see what messages you can find within yourself. Ask yourself questions like, "What can I learn from this dream?" and "How does this dream help me make sense of my life right now?" Reflection is a powerful tool for self-discovery and can help you understand any messages that Archangel Uriel sends you.

Don't Overthink It

Dreams can also often be confusing and overwhelming, so it's important not to overthink them but to try to get a balance between introspection and overwhelm. Just record the details of your dream and then let it go. Overthinking can block out any potential messages from Archangel Uriel. So just relax and trust that you'll receive the answers you need. If you're feeling stuck, take a break and return to it later.

By following these steps, you can start to unlock the power of dreamwork and connect with Archangel Uriel in a new way. So, remember to keep an open mind, trust your intuition, and surrender to the messages that come to you in your dreams. With time, patience, and practice, you'll be able to understand the deeper meanings behind the messages that Uriel is sending you.

Benefits of Dream Journaling

Dream journaling is a powerful tool for connecting with Archangel Uriel, but it has several other benefits. Keeping a dream journal can help you become more mindful, better understand your subconscious, and recognize patterns and themes in your dreams. It can also provide clarity and help give you the answers and clarity you're looking for. Here are some of the top benefits that come with dream journaling:

- **Creative Inspiration:** Dreams can serve as a great source of inspiration for writers, artists, and musicians. You can capture and explore those imaginative moments by keeping a dream journal. Who knows, you might even create something beautiful from your dreams.
- **Enhancing Your Memory**: Dreams are often forgotten within minutes of waking up. However, you can store them in your long-term memory by writing them down. This not only improves your ability to remember dreams, but it can also enhance your overall memory skills. The act of recording your dreams can also help you to better remember them.
- **Deeper Self-Reflection:** Our dreams can reveal subconscious thoughts and feelings that we may not be aware of during our waking hours. Writing down these dreams can be a way to open up those inner realms and explore them further. This can help with self-reflection and personal growth. The insights you gain can be incredibly powerful and help give you the answers you want.
- **Better Sleep:** Using a dream journal can help in getting better sleep. Writing down your dreams before bed can help release

negative thoughts and feelings from your mind, allowing you to enjoy a peaceful sleep. You can also set intentions for your dreams while journaling, which may help you have more positive and uplifting dreams.

Dream journals can offer many benefits for anyone interested in exploring their inner selves. A dream journal can be an amazing tool for understanding your dreams, finding creative inspiration, improving your memory, deepening your self-reflection, and bettering your sleep. Start your dream journal today and begin unraveling the mysteries of your subconscious mind!

Tips for Connecting with Archangel Uriel through Dreamwork

Archangel Uriel, the angel of wisdom and illumination, is here to help us connect with our inner light and see the truth in our lives. Connecting with him can be a deeply transformative experience. Here are some tips for connecting with Archangel Uriel through dreamwork.

- **Meditate before Bed:** Meditating before bed can also help you to connect with Archangel Uriel in your dreams. Before bed, take a few minutes to meditate and ask Archangel Uriel to guide you in your dreams. This will help to quiet your mind and make it easier to connect with Archangel Uriel.
- **Use Crystals:** Crystals can also be effective tools for connecting with Archangel Uriel through dreamwork. Some crystals associated with Archangel Uriel include amethyst, citrine, and clear quartz. Place these crystals under your pillow or on your nightstand before bed. They can help to amplify your connection with Archangel Uriel in your dreams.
- **Trust Your Intuition:** Trusting your intuition is key to connecting with Archangel Uriel through dreamwork. Pay attention to any gut feelings or hunches you have about your dreams. Archangel Uriel often communicates through our intuition, so it's important to trust it.

Connecting with Archangel Uriel through dreamwork can be a deeply transformative experience. Setting your intention, keeping a dream journal, meditating before bed, using crystals, and trusting your intuition are all tools that can help you to connect with him in your dreams.

Remember to be patient and trust the process, and you will soon discover the wisdom and illumination that Archangel Uriel has to offer. This chapter covered the basics of dreamwork and connecting with Archangel Uriel through it. Using the tips outlined in this chapter, you can begin to explore your dreams and connect with Archangel Uriel for answers, guidance, and healing. Happy dreaming!

Chapter 8: Crystals and Candles

Archangel Uriel is known for his association with both crystals and candles. These two elements can be powerful tools for connecting with his energy and seeking guidance. Crystals such as citrine and amber are believed to resonate with Uriel's energy and can be carried or placed on an altar. Similarly, lighting a yellow or gold candle can also invite Uriel's energy into your space. By using these tools and invoking Uriel's presence, you can tap into his wisdom and receive guidance and protection on your path.

Are you ready to tap into the awesome power of crystals and candles? Look no further than this chapter, which has got you covered on both fronts. The first sub-section delves into the fascinating world of crystal energy and how it can be channeled to connect with the Archangel Uriel. From amethyst to rose quartz, there's a crystal for every purpose and intention. The second sub-section explores how candles can communicate with the world beyond, whether to send a message to a loved one or invite positive energy. So, grab your crystals, light a candle, and let Archangel Uriel guide you.

Harnessing the Power of Crystals to Channel Uriel's Energy

Crystals can help you tap into Uriel's guidance.
https://unsplash.com/photos/bGxyxfqeq34?utm_source=unsplash&utm_medium=referral&utm_content=creditShareLink

Uriel is known for being the angel to help us connect with our inner wisdom and bring clarity to our lives. One way to channel Uriel's energy is by using crystals that resonate with his vibration. By harnessing the power of crystals, you can tap into Uriel's vast energy supply and receive guidance and illumination in your life. Whether you choose to use clear quartz, amethyst, citrine, Angelite, or lapis lazuli, each crystal has a unique vibration that calls to the Archangel on an intensely deep level.

Experiment with different crystals and see which ones resonate with you the most. With consistent practice, you'll be able to access Uriel's energy whenever you need it, bringing clarity and illumination into your life. This section will explore the power of crystals to channel Uriel's energy and how you can use them in your spiritual practice.

Hematite

Crystals have been revered for their mystical properties since ancient times, and their power to heal and restore balance to the mind, body, and spirit is growing in popularity more and more today. One such crystal that has been used for centuries is hematite, known for its grounding, protective, and transformative properties. But did you know that hematite can be used to channel the energy of Archangel Uriel? Let's explore the benefits, methods of use, cleansing, and programming techniques associated with using hematite to tap into Uriel's energy.

Benefits

The Archangel Uriel is associated with creativity, wisdom, and spiritual awakenings. According to spiritual traditions, Uriel's energy can help us overcome negative emotional patterns, dispel fear and doubt, assist with decision-making, and access intuition. Hematite, as a grounding and protective crystal, can amplify these effects by absorbing any negative energies we may be carrying and helping to balance our energy centers. By channeling Uriel's energy through hematite, we may experience greater clarity, purpose, and creative potential.

Methods of Use

There are several ways to use hematite to channel Uriel's energy. One popular method is to simply carry a piece of hematite with you throughout the day, either in your pocket, on a necklace or bracelet, or in a pouch. This allows you to stay connected to the crystal's grounding and protective energies while also inviting Uriel's wisdom and inspiration into your life.

Another technique is to meditate with hematite, holding it in your hand or placing it on your third eye or crown chakra. This can help you access Uriel's energy more directly and tune in to your spiritual insights and intuition. Finally, you can use hematite to create a crystal grid or altar, placing it alongside other crystals and symbols reflecting Uriel's energy.

Cleansing and Programming with Uriel's Energy

Like all crystals, hematite should be cleansed and programmed regularly to maintain its energetic integrity. Some methods of cleansing and programming hematite include:

- Cleansing with salt water or moonlight
- Setting intentions through meditation or visualization
- Smudging with sage or other cleansing herbs
- Placing it on a selenite charging plate
- Programming it with specific affirmations or energetic intentions related to Uriel's energy

Hematite is a crystal that carries a lot of force and has many benefits for the mind, body, and spirit. By learning how to use hematite to channel the energy of the Archangel Uriel, you can tap into its transformative power and access greater levels of intuition, creativity, and inspiration. Whether you carry a hematite with you throughout the day, meditate with it, or create a crystal grid, incorporating hematite into your spiritual practice can help you feel more balanced, grounded, and connected to your inner wisdom.

Obsidian

Obsidian is a potent spiritual tool that many cultures have used for centuries. It is a dark volcanic glass with a natural luster, making it highly sought after in jewelry and ornaments. But, perhaps the most impressive use of obsidian is its ability to channel energy. One such energy is Uriel's energy of wisdom and insight. This section will discuss the many benefits of using obsidian to channel Uriel's energy, how it can be used, and how to cleanse and program it.

Benefits

The benefits of using obsidian to channel Uriel's energy are numerous. It can help you gain clarity and insight into complex situations. As the angel of illumination and guidance, Uriel is easily summoned using this crystal and, once with you, bestows his knowledge and wisdom. Another benefit is that obsidian can enhance your intuition, allowing you to make better decisions. Finally, obsidian can help you release negative emotions, such as anger and fear, allowing you to move forward with peace.

Methods of Use

There are several ways to use obsidian to channel Uriel's energy. One popular method is to carry an obsidian stone or wear it as jewelry. This will allow you to have continuous access to Uriel's energy. Another method is to place an obsidian pyramid in your home or office, which can help to clear negative energy and promote positivity. You can also meditate with an obsidian stone, either by holding it or placing it on your third eye chakra, to connect deeply with Uriel's energy.

Cleansing and Programming with Uriel's Energy

Once you have found your obsidian stone that feels right in your hands, it's important to cleanse and program it before you use it. You can soak the stone in saltwater or place it in the sun or moonlight for a few hours to cleanse the stone. To program the stone, set an intention or affirmation for how you want to use it. For example, you can say, "I program this obsidian to help me gain insight and clarity." This will help to focus the energy of Uriel through the obsidian stone.

Connecting with Uriel's Energy

To connect with Uriel's energy, start by finding a quiet space and sitting comfortably in this space. Take several deep breaths and focus on your intention to connect with Uriel. Hold the obsidian stone or place it on your third eye chakra. Visualize a white light surrounding you and the stone. Then, simply allow yourself to receive Uriel's guidance, clarity, and wisdom.

Obsidian is a powerful spiritual tool that can channel Uriel's energy. The benefits of using obsidian to connect with this energy include gaining insight and clarity, enhancing intuition, and releasing negative emotions. There are several methods of use, including carrying or wearing the stone, placing it in your home or office, and meditating with it. To cleanse and program the stone, soak it in saltwater or place it in the sun or moonlight and set an intention for how you want to use it. Overall, using obsidian to channel Uriel's energy can bring peace and enlightenment to your life.

Tiger's Eye

Crystals are natural healers that transmit energy vibrations, and one such crystal is Tiger's Eye. This stunning golden-brown stone has been used for centuries to enhance willpower, courage, and mental clarity. The crystal's powerful vibrations are believed to help us connect with the Archangel Uriel, the angel of wisdom and prosperity.

Benefits

Tiger's Eye is a grounding stone that can bring stability and balance to our lives. It is excellent for dispelling fears and boosting our self-confidence. When we use Tiger's Eye to connect with Uriel, we experience heightened mental clarity and focus. Uriel's energy is known to help us gain deep insights into any situation, and Tiger's Eye can amplify this energy, making it easier for us to channel it. Additionally, this crystal can help us connect with our inner strength, giving us the courage to pursue our goals and dreams.

Methods of Use

There are several ways to use Tiger's Eye to channel Uriel's energy. One of the most effective is to hold the crystal in our hands and focus on the intention of connecting with Uriel. We can also place the stone on our third eye chakra to enhance intuition and inner wisdom. Another way is to wear the crystal as jewelry in the form of a bracelet or necklace, allowing its energy to work on us continuously throughout the day. Lastly, we can also meditate with the crystal, holding it in our hands and focusing on our breath, allowing the crystal's natural vibrations to calm our minds and bodies.

Cleansing and Programming with Uriel's Energy

Cleaning and programming your crystal with Uriel's energy is essential to ensure it works properly. Cleansing the crystal can be done by placing it in a bowl of filtered water and leaving it out in the moonlight or sunlight for a few hours. Programming the crystal can be done by holding it in your hands and reciting a prayer or affirmation, asking Uriel to infuse the crystal with his energy. This step ensures that the crystal's energy is in alignment with our intentions and desires.

Tiger's Eye is a powerful and versatile crystal that can help us connect with Uriel's energy to enhance our spiritual growth and mental clarity. It can bring balance and stability to our lives and give us the courage to pursue our goals and dreams. The use of Tiger's Eye can help us tune in to Uriel's energy, making it easier for us to receive insights and guidance from the angel of wisdom and prosperity. With proper cleansing and programming, Tiger's Eye can become a constant source of comfort and healing, contributing to our overall well-being.

Amber

Have you ever heard of the healing properties of amber? This beautiful golden gemstone formed from the sap of ancient trees is more than just a pretty piece of jewelry. Amber is believed to have incredible healing abilities, and when paired with the powerful energy of Archangel Uriel, it can have a profound effect on your mind, body, and spirit.

Benefits

Amber carries warm, comforting energy to help soothe anxiety, fear, and depression. The stone is also believed to have anti-inflammatory properties, making it useful for various physical ailments, including joint pain, osteoarthritis, and rheumatoid arthritis. In addition, Uriel's energy helps us to let go of negative emotions, boosts our intuition, and promotes clarity of thought. Using amber to channel Uriel's energy, we tap into his wisdom and gain a deeper understanding of ourselves and our path in life.

Methods of Use

There are many ways to use amber to channel Uriel's energy. One of the simplest ways is to wear an amber necklace, bracelet, or earrings. As you wear the stone, you can focus your intention on calling in Uriel's energy, allowing it to flow through the stone and into your body. Another popular method is to meditate with an amber stone. Hold the stone, close your eyes, and focus on your breath. As you inhale, visualize golden light flowing into your body, carrying the energy of Uriel with it. As you exhale, release any negative emotions or thoughts which no longer serve you.

Cleansing and Programming with Uriel's Energy

To enhance the healing powers of your amber, keep it cleansed and programmed with the energy of Uriel at all times. To do this, you can hold the stone in your hand and focus your intention on clearing any negative energy from it. You can also visualize a beam of golden light flowing into the stone, infusing it with Uriel's energy. Once your amber is cleansed, it's time to program it with your intention. Hold the stone in your hand and visualize what you want to manifest in your life. It could be anything from financial abundance to emotional healing. As you visualize your intention, allow Uriel's energy to flow through the stone, amplifying your manifestation power.

Using amber has a powerful effect on your physical, emotional, and spiritual well-being. By wearing amber jewelry, meditating with an amber stone, and cleansing and programming it with the energy of Uriel, you can tap into a powerful source of healing and illumination. Remember that intention is key when using amber to channel Uriel's energy. Set your intention clearly and focus your energy on it with trust and faith. As you practice working with Amber and Uriel's energy, you may find your intuition, inner wisdom, and sense of purpose becoming clearer and stronger, leading you to a more fulfilling and joyful life.

Enhance Your Meditation Experience with Crystals

Welcome to a world of serenity, balance, and peace, where the healing powers of crystals will help you achieve a true state of mindfulness and meditation. This section will explore how you can use crystals to channel Uriel's divine energy to help you unlock your inner self, enhance your meditation experience, and connect with the universe. Whether you are a seasoned meditator or a novice, this will help you explore the power of crystals and tap into Uriel's divine energy using simple yet powerful exercises.

Crystals have been used for spiritual, physical, and emotional healing for centuries. They possess unique vibrational frequencies that can interact with your energy field, helping you to achieve better health, emotional balance, and spiritual growth. The key to unlocking their power during meditation is to choose crystals that resonate with Uriel's energy. Clear quartz, citrine, carnelian, and garnet are all crystals associated with Uriel's energy, and they possess unique properties that can help you connect with his divine energy.

The Basics

To use crystals to meditate with Uriel's energy, start by finding a quiet, safe space where you can meditate without distractions. Sit comfortably with your chosen crystal in your hand, or place it over your heart. Close your eyes, take deep breaths, and visualize Uriel's energy as a golden light entering your body from above. Focus on the crystal's energy, feel its vibrations, and let its energy flow through your body, starting from your head and going right down to your toes. Breathe deeply, release any tension, and let yourself be guided by Uriel's divine energy.

Crystal Grid

Using a crystal grid is another way to connect with Uriel's energy during meditation. This geometric shape is created by placing crystals in a specific pattern on a surface. To create a crystal grid for meditation, start by choosing crystals that correspond to Uriel's energy, such as clear quartz, carnelian, and garnet. Place the crystals in a pattern of your choice, focusing on their placement and intention. Once you have created the grid, sit in front of it and focus on Uriel's energy, visualizing it flowing through the crystals and into your body.

Meditation Necklace

You can use crystals to create a meditation necklace if you want a more attractive meditation exercise. A meditation necklace is made of crystals chosen based on their energy and vibrational frequency. To make the necklace, use crystals that resonate with Uriel's energy, selecting beads of clear quartz, carnelian, and garnet. String them on a cord, focusing on the intention of the necklace to help you connect with Uriel's energy during meditation. Wear the necklace during meditation, allowing the crystals' vibrations to enhance your experience.

The Magic of Candle Work and Uriel's Energy

There's just something about the flicker of a candle that brings a sense of peace and tranquility to a troubled soul. From the soft glow of a birthday candle to the warmth of a candlelit dinner, candles have been used for centuries to create ambiance and set the mood. But did you know that candles can also be used to set intentions, unlock your inner magic, and connect with your spiritual side? This section will explore the world of candle work and the powerful energy of Archangel Uriel.

What Is Candle Work?

Candle work is the practice of using candles to manifest your desires and intentions. Each candle color corresponds with a different intention or energy. For example, green candles are often used for abundance and prosperity, while purple candles are used for spiritual growth and intuition. By lighting a candle with a specific intention, you can focus your energy and bring that intention to fruition.

Combining Candle Work with Uriel's Energy

You can use this combination of a colored candle and Uriel's energy to help with any area of your life, whether career, relationships, or personal growth. But how do you go about combining candle work and Uriel's energy?

Simply light a candle in the color that corresponds with your intention and ask Uriel to be present with you. You can speak your intention aloud or simply hold it in your mind. As you focus on your intention, imagine Uriel's energy surrounding you and providing you with guidance and clarity. Another way to incorporate Uriel's energy into your candle work is by using specific candles that are infused with Uriel's energy. These candles are often charged with crystals and essential oils that correspond with Uriel's energy, making them even more powerful. You can find these candles online or at local metaphysical stores.

Candle Colors and Their Healing Associations

Candles have been used as a form of healing for centuries. They emit a warm glow that has therapeutic effects on the mind, body, and soul. Each candle color represents a unique energy vibration that helps us achieve our desired outcome. Additionally, calling upon an archangel like Uriel can amplify the energy and power of the candle. This section will delve into the associations of different candle colors, their healing properties, and how Uriel can enhance the energy to help us manifest our desires.

- **White Candles:** White candles represent purity and a higher power. They can be used for protection, guidance, and clearing negative influences. To enhance the white candle's energy, call upon Archangel Uriel for guidance and protection.
- **Yellow Candles:** Yellow candles are associated with mental clarity, communication, and self-confidence. They can enhance focus, improve memory, and relieve anxiety. Call Archangel Uriel for mental clarity and guidance to enhance the yellow candle's energy.
- **Green Candles:** Green candles represent abundance, wealth, and prosperity. They can be used to manifest good fortune, health, and wealth. To enhance the green candle's energy, call upon Archangel Uriel for abundance, prosperity, and growth.
- **Blue Candles**: Blue candles represent calm, serenity, and tranquility. They can calm an overactive mind, relieve stress, and promote relaxation. To enhance the blue candle's energy, call upon Archangel Uriel for calm and peace.
- **Red Candles:** Red candles represent passion, strength, and courage. They can attract love, enhance sexuality, and increase vitality. Call upon Archangel Uriel for strength and courage to enhance the red candle's energy.
- **Purple Candles:** Purple candles represent spirituality, meditation, and psychic ability. They can enhance intuition, psychic abilities, and spiritual enlightenment. Call upon Archangel Uriel for spiritual guidance and enlightenment to

enhance the purple candle's energy.

- **Black Candles:** Black candles represent protection, banishing, and grounding. They can be used for clearing negativity, protection from malicious energies, and grounding. To enhance the black candle's energy, call upon Archangel Uriel for protection and grounding.

Using candles as a healing tool can be an easy and effective method to manifest our intentions. The energy vibration of each color can help us align with our desires, and calling upon Archangel Uriel can elevate and amplify the energy. Using the practical list of candle colors and their associations, we can be more intentional with our candle selection and create a powerful and transformative healing experience. Remember, working with candles is a form of self-care, and by taking time for ourselves, we can create a more positive and fulfilling life.

Channeling Uriel's Energy with Candle Meditation and Visualization

Do you ever feel emotionally or mentally drained? Do you struggle to remain focused or find inner peace amidst the chaos of daily life? Perhaps it's time to tap into the power of meditation and visualization. By focusing our thoughts and energy, we can connect with the divine and receive the guidance and strength we need. Let's explore the art of candle meditation and visualization exercises, specifically focused on channeling the energy of Archangel Uriel.

1. The first step in candle meditation is to find a quiet, calm space. Sit comfortably on the floor or in a chair with your spine erect and your eyes closed. Take a few deep breaths and focus your thoughts on Uriel. Begin visualizing him before you, glowing with light and wisdom. Allow his energy to envelop you, protecting and guiding you.

2. Next, light a candle in front of you. Watch the flame, focusing your attention solely on its movements. If your mind wanders, gently redirect your thoughts back to the flame. As you watch the fire flicker, visualize Uriel's energy connecting with you, bringing you clarity and insight. You may even wish to recite a mantra like "Uriel, fill me with your wisdom."

3. As you continue to gaze at the candle, visualize Uriel's energy flowing into the flame and then back into you. Imagine the energy filling up your body, from the crown of your head to the soles of your feet. Feel it cleansing and purifying you, washing away any negativity or doubt. Allow yourself to bask in the warmth and light of Uriel's energy, knowing that you are protected and guided.
4. Imagine yourself surrounded by a golden bubble of light. Picture the bubble growing larger and larger until it encompasses your entire room. Imagine Uriel's energy guiding you, inspiring you, and infusing you with his wisdom inside the bubble. Feel the energy pulsing through you, empowering you to move forward with confidence and clarity.
5. Thank Uriel for his guidance and protection. Visualize his energy lifting you out of your meditation, helping you to feel renewed and refreshed. Affirm to yourself that you are worthy of abundance, joy, and wisdom and that you will continue to channel Uriel's energy as you move through your day.

By practicing candle meditation and visualization exercises, we can tap into Archangel Uriel's power and connect with our inner wisdom. These practices help us to remain calm and centered, even amid life's challenges. Remember to take time for yourself daily, even just a few minutes, to practice these exercises and connect with the divine. You'll be amazed at the clarity and insight that you can gain.

This chapter has explored how crystals and candles can help us channel Archangel Uriel's energy. Using crystals and candles as a form of self-care is a great way to foster positive energy, clarity, and insight. Crystals vibrate at various frequencies, which activate our chakras and bring balance to our energetic field. Candles can enhance our emotional state by promoting relaxation and providing a calming atmosphere. Lastly, candle meditation and visualization exercises can help us connect with Uriel's energy, gaining clarity and insight.

Chapter 9: Daily Rituals and Exercises

Are you looking to connect more deeply with Archangel Uriel? Incorporating daily rituals and exercises into your routine can help establish a strong spiritual connection with this archangel known for his wisdom and guidance. Try setting aside some quiet time each morning to meditate and call upon Archangel Uriel for guidance throughout the day. This chapter will set out step-by-step instructions on creating a daily practice that will help enhance your connection with Archangel Uriel and be simple enough to add to your daily routine. Each section will also detail various exercises, meditations, and affirmations that you can use to re-energize your spiritual connection. By prioritizing these daily rituals, you'll be on your way to building a stronger relationship with this powerful archangel.

Enhancing Creativity through Archangel Uriel

Creativity is a gift, but it's not always easy to tap into. During times of stress or burnout, accessing the creative part of our minds can be even more challenging. However, with the help of Archangel Uriel, we can unlock our imagination and bring our ideas to life. Here's a step-by-step guide for enhancing creativity with the guidance of Archangel Uriel.

Daily Exercises

Daily exercise can allow you to tap into your creativity.
https://unsplash.com/photos/WvDYdXDzkhs?utm_source=unsplash&utm_medium=referral&utm_content=creditShareLink

Creating a daily exercise routine can enhance your creativity. Archangel Uriel guides us to focus our energy on the present moment, which helps us relax and focus on the task at hand. One way to do this is through movement. Activities such as yoga, dance, or even a simple walk can help you clear your head and bring inspiration to your projects. You can also try free writing, where you write down your thoughts for a few minutes each day. This will help you identify patterns and themes that may spark new ideas.

Meditations

Archangel Uriel is known for guiding us to our inner wisdom. Meditation is a potent tool to access that wisdom and creativity within ourselves. Begin by sitting silently for a few minutes each day, focusing on your breath and allowing your mind to quiet. As you breathe, imagine a white light surrounding you, inviting Archangel Uriel to join you. You can also try guided meditations specifically designed for creativity. These meditations often take you on a journey to discover new ideas or perspectives.

Affirmations

Affirmations are another powerful way to shift your mindset towards a more positive and creative outlook. Start by choosing three affirmations related to creativity, such as "I am a vessel for divine inspiration" or "My creativity flows effortlessly." Repeat these affirmations to yourself each day, either in meditation or as an intentional thought throughout your day. You can also create vision boards with images and quotes that inspire you.

Access Wisdom and Mental Clarity with Archangel Uriel

Feeling lost, confused, or overwhelmed by life's challenges can take a mental and emotional toll. Fortunately, there are spiritual helpers who we can call for guidance, wisdom, and mental clarity. The guide that this book concentrates on is the Archangel Uriel, the angel of wisdom and illumination. With a little practice, anyone can learn to access Uriel's divine assistance to improve the quality of their lives. Here's a step-by-step guide on accessing the wisdom and mental clarity you need through Archangel Uriel.

Daily Exercises

One of the best ways to access Uriel's wisdom is through daily exercises that help you connect with your intuition and inner guidance. You can easily incorporate these exercises into your daily routine, such as taking 10-15 minutes each morning or night to practice deep breathing and mindfulness meditation, journaling, or simply sitting in silence and letting your thoughts drift.

Meditations

Find a quiet, peaceful place to sit and begin by visualizing the divine light and warmth of Archangel Uriel surrounding you. Focus on your breath and allow any thoughts or emotions to simply pass by like clouds in the sky. As you tune into your breath and the present moment, ask Uriel for guidance, clarity, and wisdom. You may receive a message or impression or simply feel a sense of peace and comfort.

Affirmations

These positive statements can help change your mentality and bring about positive change in your life. Some examples of affirmations you can use to connect with Archangel Uriel include "I am open to receiving divine guidance and wisdom," "I trust that the universe has a plan for me," and "I am filled with peace, love, and clarity."

Nature Walks

Connecting with nature is a great way to access Uriel's wisdom and tap into your intuition. You can take a walk in the park, go hiking, or simply sit outside in your backyard or balcony. As you immerse yourself in the natural beauty around you, ask Uriel for guidance and clarity on any issues or questions. You may find that the answers come more easily than expected.

Healing from Traumas

Whether physical or emotional, trauma can leave deep scars in a person's psyche. They often result in fear, anxiety, and depression – significantly affecting your quality of life. Archangel Uriel's divine guidance can provide a unique path toward healing for people struggling to find a way out of their trauma. Known as the "light of God," Archangel Uriel's healing energy helps release emotional wounds and transform one's life. Here's a step-by-step process to help you heal from trauma with Archangel Uriel.

Daily Exercises

The first step in this journey of self-healing is to take care of your physical health. Start by incorporating daily exercises such as yoga, meditation, or walking into your routine. These activities will bring balance to your mind, body, and spirit, and you will feel relaxed and energized simultaneously. If you prefer intense physical activities like running or weightlifting, go ahead and do those. Whatever you choose to do, be consistent. Physical activity has been shown to lower levels of stress hormones like cortisol and adrenaline, which can trigger anxiety and hyperarousal in traumas.

Meditations

Now that you've incorporated healthy habits into your daily routine, you will move on to meditation. Meditation can help calm the noise in your mind and release negativity. With Archangel Uriel's divine energy, meditations can become a transformative experience that helps you release the toxic energy trapped within you. Start your meditation with deep breaths, inhale through your nose, and exhale through your mouth. Visualize the divine light of Archangel Uriel surrounding you like a warm blanket. You can also visualize yourself in nature, surrounded by trees, rivers, or mountains. This visualization will help you connect with the divine energy and release any pain, fear, or sadness.

Affirmations

The other powerful tool that can help you heal from trauma is affirmations. Words have power, and when you speak them frequently, they become a part of your subconscious thoughts. Affirmations are positive statements you repeatedly say to yourself to remind yourself that you are worthy of love, healing, and happiness. With Archangel Uriel's powerful energy, affirmations become even more potent and effective. Choose positive affirmations that resonate with you, and recite them throughout the day. Examples of affirmations are "I am worthy of love and joy," "I radiate with happiness and positivity," and "I release all the fears and doubts within me."

Seeking Professional Help

While daily exercises, meditation, and affirmations might work wonders for some people, they might not be enough to heal from severe trauma. Remember, it's okay to seek professional help if you feel that you need it. A professional therapist or counselor can help you navigate your emotions and guide you through a healthy path toward healing. Archangel Uriel's energy will always be with you, and seeking professional help will not hinder the process but accelerate it.

Raising Your Vibration

Have you ever felt that everything around you is just slightly off? Maybe you can't shake the feeling of negativity, or you just can't seem to find your happiness. The solution might lie in raising your vibration. When we have a high vibration, we attract more positive experiences, people, and opportunities into our lives. One way to raise your vibration is by working with Archangel Uriel. Here's a step-by-step guide on how to raise your vibration through Archangel Uriel.

Daily Exercises

One way to raise your vibration is through daily exercise that will promote positivity and self-care. For example, you can start or end your day with an uplifting yoga routine or take a meditative walk in nature. When you make time for activities that bring joy to your life, you naturally increase your vibration. The key is prioritizing your happiness and making it a habit to care for your mind, body, and soul.

Meditations

Meditation is a powerful tool for connecting with Archangel Uriel and raising your vibration. Begin by finding a quiet space to sit comfortably and focus on breathing. Once you feel centered, visualize yourself surrounded by a bright, golden light. This light represents Archangel Uriel's uplifting energy. Feel the warmth of his energy and allow it to fill your heart space. When you're ready, silently ask him for guidance and support. Trust that He is always with you, and His energy will help you manifest your highest potential.

Affirmations

Affirmations can help you reprogram your subconscious mind and raise your vibration. You can begin by creating a list of affirmations that resonate with you. Some examples include, "I am deserving of love and happiness," or "I trust the process of my life." Once you have your list, recite these affirmations to yourself every day. You can say them in your head or out loud. The key is to embody the energy of the affirmation and fully believe in its truth.

Self-Reflection

Taking a step back and reflecting on your life occasionally is crucial. Ask yourself what experiences or emotions are holding you back from manifesting your ideal life. Acknowledge them, and then release them with the help of Archangel Uriel. You can do this through a visualization technique. See yourself placing these limiting beliefs in a bubble and surrendering them to Uriel's energy. Trust that he will help transmute these beliefs into positivity and light.

Writing to Archangel Uriel

If you're seeking peace, wisdom, and divine guidance, Archangel Uriel is here to help. This mighty being of light radiates calm, tranquility, and deep insight and can help you overcome obstacles, heal old wounds, and manifest your dreams. One of the powerful ways to connect with Uriel is by putting your thoughts, fears, hopes, and intentions on paper. This way, you can tap into your inner wisdom, release negative energies, and receive powerful messages from the angel realm. Here's a step-by-step guide to show you how to write to Archangel Uriel in a clear, focused, and effective way to receive the guidance and blessings you seek.

Step 1: Prepare Your Space

Before you begin writing, setting the stage for your communication with Archangel Uriel is important. Find a quiet, comfortable space where you won't be disturbed. Light a candle, burn some incense or sage, and play soft music if you like. You can also create an altar or a special place for Uriel by placing crystals, flowers, feathers, or other sacred objects that resonate with you. Take a few deep breaths, center yourself, and ask Archangel Uriel to be with you, guide you, and protect you as you write.

Step 2: State Your Intention

Once you've prepared your space, take a moment to clarify your intention for writing to Archangel Uriel. Do you seek clarity on a specific issue? Do you want to release old patterns, fears, or doubts? Or do you simply want to deepen your connection with the divine? Write your intention clearly and concisely, and let it guide your writing. You can begin with a simple statement, such as "Dear Archangel Uriel, I am writing to you today because…" or "I ask for your guidance on the matter of…"

Step 3: Pour Your Heart Out

Now it's time to let your words flow freely and openly. Don't worry about grammar, spelling, or structure; just write from your heart and soul. If you feel stuck or overwhelmed, you can start with some prompts or questions, such as:

- What are my deepest fears about this situation?
- What are my highest aspirations and hopes?
- What do I need to let go of to move forward?
- What actions or steps can I take to align with my purpose?

As you write, allow yourself to express whatever comes up for you without judgment or self-censorship. You can also address Archangel Uriel directly as if you were having a conversation with a wise and compassionate friend. Remember that Uriel is here to help you, to guide you, and to love you unconditionally.

Step 4: Express Your Gratitude

Once you've written down what you wanted to convey, it is important to end with a simple expression of gratitude towards Archangel Uriel. This act of gratitude opens up the connection between the archangel

Uriel and the person who is writing the letter.

Step 5: Keep Your Writing Safe

Don't forget to keep your writing in a special place when finished. You may want to read it after a while to see how you have progressed in your journey and the lessons learned or guide yourself through future challenges.

Following these simple steps, you can create a powerful and transformative dialogue with Archangel Uriel through writing. Whether you need comfort, guidance, healing, or inspiration, Uriel is always there for you, ready to support you on your path. Remember that writing is a powerful tool for self-discovery, empowerment, and co-creation with the universe.

The daily rituals and exercises provided in this chapter can help you foster a deeper connection with Uriel and receive his guidance and blessings. As always, be sure to thank him for all he has done for you! May the love of Uriel fill your life with joy, inspiration, and purpose!

Bonus: Correspondences Sheet

Archangel Uriel is known for his incredible ability to help us find our way through challenges and bring clarity to our lives. There are certain correspondences associated with Uriel which can help us better connect and understand his energy. This bonus sheet includes a chart outlining all of the correspondences related to Archangel Uriel. It will serve as a great reference for anyone looking to understand more about this powerful and compassionate archangel. Use this chart as a quick reference to help you connect with Archangel Uriel's energy!

Day Of The Week	Saturday
Hour Of The Day	8 am
Festivals/Feasts Of The Year	1. Feast of St. Michael and All Angels (September 29th) 2. Feast of St. Gabriel (March 24th) 3. Feast of the Nativity of St. John the Baptist (June 24th)
Zodiac Sign And Planet	Leo, the Sun
Angel Number	888

Direction	East
Element	Fire
Colors	Gold, White, and Orange
Symbol/Seal/Sigil	Six-pointed star
Trees, Plants, And Herbs/Oils	Myrrh, Marigold, and Carnation
Crystal(s) And Metal(s)	Citrine, Amber, and Gold

Archangel Uriel is an incredibly powerful archangel who can provide us with the guidance, clarity, and insight we need to move forward in our lives. Correspondences associated with this powerful angel include the colors gold, white, and orange, which are often associated with enlightenment and positivity. Crystals like citrine and amber are also often linked to Uriel's energy, as they connect us with his guidance and bring more light into our lives.

Fire is another element closely associated with Archangel Uriel and carries the energy of transformation, allowing us to become more enlightened and emotionally stable. Similarly, myrrh, marigolds, and carnations can be used to help us connect with Uriel's energy. These plants are often used in healing spells and rituals, helping to bring clarity and understanding into our lives.

The feast of St. Michael and All Angels (September 29th) is also linked to Uriel's energy, so taking the time to honor this day can be a powerful way to connect with him and thank him for his guidance. Meditating with Archangel Uriel's sigil or seal can help us open up to his energy and create a strong connection with him. Calling on Uriel during times of uncertainty or confusion can be a powerful way to gain much-needed insight and understanding. Through his guidance, we can find the courage to move forward and overcome any obstacle in our path.

By aligning ourselves with these spiritual correspondences associated with Archangel Uriel, we can create a strong connection with his energy and invite more understanding, clarity, and enlightenment into our lives.

Conclusion

When it comes to the divine realm, there are few beings as powerful and awe-inspiring as Archangel Uriel. This celestial being is known for the incredible light and love that he brings into the world, spreading joy and positivity wherever he goes. Whether you're seeking guidance, protection, or simply a sense of peace and tranquility, Uriel is there to help you tap into your inner strength and discover your true potential. With his boundless energy and unwavering commitment to goodness, Uriel is a beacon of hope and inspiration for us all. If you're ever feeling lost or alone, just know that Archangel Uriel is watching over you, ready to offer compassion and support whenever you need it most.

In times of uncertainty and confusion, Archangel Uriel shines a light on the path to our truest selves. As the angel of wisdom, clarity, and truth, Uriel helps us see through the fog of doubt and insecurity to find the answers inside us all along. Whether it's uncovering our passion for a new career or realizing the depth of our love for someone special, Uriel's guidance can lead us to fulfilling our deepest desires and dreams.

When we have Archangel Uriel on our side, there's no limit to what we can achieve. With His divine wisdom guiding us, we can trust in our ability to make the right decisions and confidently move forward. Uriel brings a sense of clarity that is reassuring and empowering, allowing us to see situations in a new light and approach them with renewed vigor. Whether facing challenges or pursuing our dreams, Uriel is there to lend us his strength and support.

This guide has explored ways to connect with Archangel Uriel. From creating angelic sacred space and performing solar chakra meditations to using crystals and candles for divination, these rituals and exercises will help you open your heart, mind, and spirit to the presence of this powerful angel. If you're ever feeling overwhelmed or unsure of which direction to take in life, simply call upon Uriel, and you will soon be filled with the strength and courage needed to move forward.

The accompanying Correspondences Sheet with this guide contains helpful symbols and affirmations associated with Archangel Uriel. With these tools, you can deepen your connection to the angelic realm and invoke his powerful presence in times of need. The more you practice, the closer you will become to Uriel and his divine wisdom, enabling you to unlock your potential and lead a life of joy and abundance.

So, let's take this journey with Archangel Uriel and be blessed with his divine energy, wisdom, and guidance!

Here's another book by Mari Silva that you might like

Your Free Gift
(only available for a limited time)

Thanks for getting this book! If you want to learn more about various spirituality topics, then join Mari Silva's community and get a free guided meditation MP3 for awakening your third eye. This guided meditation mp3 is designed to open and strengthen ones third eye so you can experience a higher state of consciousness. Simply visit the link below the image to get started.

https://spiritualityspot.com/meditation

References

Brown, S. (2017, September 20). Who is Archangel Uriel? The Black Feather Intuitive. https://www.theblackfeatherintuitive.com/archangel-uriel/

Hopler, W. (2011, June 5). Meet Archangel Uriel, angel of wisdom. Learn Religions. https://www.learnreligions.com/meet-archangel-uriel-angel-of-wisdom-124717

Jensen, E. (2022, January 4). Archangel Uriel - angel of truth spiritual symbolism. IPublishing. https://www.ipublishing.co.in/archangel-uriel

Kalu, M. (2021, January 11). Who is the archangel, Uriel? Christianity.com. https://www.christianity.com/wiki/angels-and-demons/who-is-the-archangel-uriel.html

Varnell, J. R. (2016). Uriel. Createspace Independent Publishing Platform.

What is the role of the archangel Uriel in human life? (2020, April 20). Andija Store. https://andija.com/useful-articles/what-is-the-role-of-the-archangel-uriel-in-human-life/

Wille. (2021, January 15). Who is Archangel Uriel? The Angel of Truth. A Little Spark of Joy. https://www.alittlesparkofjoy.com/archangel-uriel

Milton Keynes UK
Ingram Content Group UK Ltd.
UKHW052002270324
440282UK00005B/52